CORPORATE GOAD

CORPORATE
GOAD

CASE STUDIES IN
TRANSFORMATIONAL
CHANGE

KURT KRAUSS

IDEAPRESS
PUBLISHING

PROUDLY PRINTED IN THE UNITED STATES OF AMERICA

Library of Congress Information

ISBN: 978-1-940858-64-7

E-book ISBN: 978-1-940858-65-4

Mind-Boggling One-Minute Mysteries and Brain Teasers

© 2010 by Sandy Silverthorne and John Warner

Published by Harvest House Publishers

Eugene, Oregon 97402

Used by permission

For information, contact the author at kkrauss1@yahoo.com.
IdeaPress books are available at a special discount for bulk purchases for
use in corporate training sessions and academic settings.
For more details, e-mail info@ideapress.com.

No animals were harmed in the writing, printing, or distribution of this
book. The trees, unfortunately, were not so lucky.

Dedication

This book is dedicated to my former Operations practice partners at Booz Allen Hamilton: Carl Blonkvist, John Devereaux, Steve Griffiths, Ed Gulas, John Houlihan, Frank Jones, Tom Jones, Roy King, Dan Lewis, Bob Mayer, Horst Metz, Randy Myer, Gary Neilson, Keith Oliver, John Piepgras, Bill Reed, Dan Riley, Gary Shows, and Alec Weight.

It was my pleasure and good fortune to work with this group of like-minded corporate goads. Individually and collectively, they are the smartest, most capable, and most accomplished professionals that I know.

CONTENTS

INTRODUCTION

It is not necessary to change. Survival is not mandatory.
—W. EDWARDS DEMING

One evening, my partner Stephen Baum and I, and our wives, were at a black-tie charitable event in New York City. We were having dinner at a table with maybe six other people and the conversation was lively. A very nice lady with very expensive jewelry asked Stephen, "So what do you do?"

"Well," he said, "I tell stories."

"You do what?"

"I tell stories."

"To whom do you tell these stories?"

"Mostly CEOs of very large companies."

"What kind of stories do you tell them?"

"Oh, stories about how other companies have succeeded or failed, and why that happened, and how the CEO might replicate or avoid such an outcome."

"And do you get paid to tell these stories?"

"Oh, yes," Stephen replied, "I get paid handsomely."

Then the nice lady with the expensive jewelry turned her attention to me. "And what about you?" she asked. "What do you do?"

"I'm a Corporate Goad," I said. "I also meet with CEOs of large companies, but instead of telling them stories, I stick my finger in their eye."

"Why on earth do you do that?"

"To get them to do things they really don't want to do, even though they know deep down that they should."

"And I suppose they pay you too," she offered.

I nodded. "Handsomely."

That was a fun evening and I have no idea what the nice lady with the expensive jewelry thought of us. But it did give us a hell of a story to tell, and it provided the title for this book: *Corporate Goad*.

✳

I spent my entire professional career as a change agent. I began in 1971 in the Production Control Department at Industrial Nucleonics Corporation in Columbus, Ohio. At that time, the field of production and inventory management was undergoing a massive transformation, enabled by the increasing availability and power of the computer. The company was truly at the leading edge of this functional transformation, and I had the opportunity to be right in the middle of it.

In 1974, I was offered the job of Production Control Manager at DAB Industries in Bellefontaine, Ohio, a manufacturer of engine bearings for the auto industry. I was brought in to upgrade the capability, expertise, and performance of the production control function. We implemented new tools to better plan, schedule, and control production. Over three years, we made many changes which resulted in significant reductions to inventories, lead times, and labor costs.

About this time, I began to get a sense of my likely career path, and I didn't like where things were headed. I knew I wanted more out of my career, and therefore, I decided to get an MBA. In 1977, Carnegie Mellon University in Pittsburgh was the third-ranked business school in the country, behind Harvard and Stanford. Not only did I get accepted by CMU, but I was able to negotiate a semester's worth of credit for my past experience. This meant that I only had to complete three semesters of course work to graduate.

In the summer before I was to start my studies, I received a call from the management consulting firm of Booz Allen Hamilton. They wanted to talk with me about joining the Operations practice in their Cleveland office, and I agreed to meet.

After interviews with at least eight people, I met with Jack McGrath, the Managing Partner of the Cleveland office. After we talked for about forty-five minutes, Jack offered me a job. Based on my understanding of management consulting, I thought that this was exactly what I wanted to do. But I also felt that I should first get my MBA.

"Jack," I said, "I'm honored to have been given an offer to join the firm, but I'm afraid that I'm going to have to turn it down. You see, I am starting an MBA program in September."

Jack began to get excited. It turns out that 95% of the successful folks at Booz Allen had an MBA. "What school?" he asked.

"Carnegie Mellon University," I replied.

"Unbelievable!" Jack said. "That's where I went to business school."

Jack extended me an offer right then to join the firm in May 1978, after my first year of school. Then I could take a leave of absence, return to school for four months in September to finish my degree, and then rejoin the firm in January 1979.

I joined the firm as an Associate in May 1978. Over the next four years, I was promoted to Senior Associate and Principal, and I was elected to the partnership in October 1984. I led the Service Operations practice from its inception in 1985 and served on the firm's board of directors from 1987 to 1991.

In 1992, I decided that it was time to leave Booz Allen. When I resigned, I had no idea what I wanted to do next. I just knew that I couldn't stay at Booz Allen. Ultimately, I decided to team up with my partners, Stephen Baum and John Smith, and form a consulting firm to be called The Mead Point Group. We would focus on operations, organization, and strategy work for service-based industries.

Over the next five years, I had more fun, was more professionally challenged, and made a lot more money than at any other time in my career. We were fortunate to have relationships with some terrific clients, some of whom followed us from Booz Allen (e.g., AT&T and Marriott) and some of whom were new to us (e.g., IBM and Young & Rubicam).

In the mid-1990s, Burson-Marsteller was the largest public relations and marketing communications firm in the world, and the largest subsidiary of advertising giant Young & Rubicam. Y&R became my client in 1993, and by 1995, I was devoting half of my time to Burson-Marsteller. I worked with CEO Larry Snoddon to improve the performance of the organization and increase profit margins, and later with the next CEO, Tom Bell, to redefine the core value proposition of the firm and align the organization with it.

In 1997, Tom said: "I want to acquire The Mead Point Group." He said that his goal was to marry together marketing communication and public relations with strategic management consulting, in the belief that both would be stronger as a result. After numerous discussions with my partners and some serious negotiations with Tom, we finally came to a deal. We closed in October 1997, thus starting a new phase of my career.

Shortly after we closed the deal, a disaster hit: Burson discovered financial fraud in Asia. This was six months before Young & Rubicam had planned to go public. The timing could not have been worse. I was asked to meet with Tom Bell and Y&R's CEO, Peter Georgescu, several days after the discovery. They told me that they needed me to take over as Chief Financial Officer of Burson-Marsteller. After considerable discussion, I agreed to take the job.

The next three years were a blast. I built a strong financial team. We fixed all of the issues surrounding the fraud, and put in controls so that it couldn't happen again. We implemented new financial and operating systems around the world. We streamlined processes. And we worked with management to improve client staff utilization, which led to improving EBITDA margins in the U.S. from 12% to 28% in just over two years.

It was a hell of a run. While management consulting was my professional calling, the three years I spent as CFO of Burson-Marsteller were the best of my career. In 1998, we took Y&R public, and in 2000, we sold the agency for $4.7 billion to the WPP Group. After speaking with my wife, I decided to retire and did so on October 3, 2000, the day after we closed the WPP deal and six days before my fifty-first birthday.

For the first few years of my retirement, I continued to do some part-time consulting work with a few past clients and colleagues. Some of these initiatives are also described in later chapters.

The reality of all my experience as a change agent was that I had to persuade people and companies to do things that they really didn't want to do, either because they were scary or risky or too difficult or politically unpopular. I had to coax them or scare them or otherwise compel them to change. I had to make them *believe*. And what fun it was! Just call me The Goad.

SETTING THE STAGE

Businesses change all the time. All you need to do is read the headlines: "Nonprofit Hospitals Face Serious Cuts," "Wal-Mart Tests Next Small Thing," "JetBlue to Reduce Capacity to Cuba." Or look around your local mall: stores opening, stores closing, "Now Hiring" signs. Yes, change is pervasive. Why, you ask? Because, very simply stated: organizations are either getting better or they're losing ground. All of them. All the time.

This is a book about real-life examples of successful, transformational changes I helped to implement across a wide variety of businesses and industries: factories, warehouses, retail stores, restaurants, hotel chains, banks, hospitals, cruise lines, and many others. I have attempted to put the case studies into a broader context and to generalize various lessons learned.

The book is not an academic treatise. There are few references and the bibliography is short. Instead, it is a book of real change initiatives that I have led, or participated in, over my career. As such, it is bounded by my experience. I've seen and done a lot, but I've not seen and done it all. My career was rooted in operations strategy in both manufacturing industries and service industries. Thus, many of the examples of successful change initiatives cited herein concern various aspects of operations management. There are some, but fewer, examples involving sales, marketing, and finance.

Corporate Goad is organized into three sections. "The Change Agent's Handbook" suggests the *sine qua non* for successfully leading corporate change: from building disciples and getting their attention to defining the problem and developing solutions.

"The Change Agent's Tool Kit" presents high-potential areas for improving business performance: extending the value proposition, aligning the organization, streamlining processes, increasing utilization, reducing complexity, and optimizing pricing.

"The Change Agent's Destiny," subtitled "The Patient-Focused Hospital, a Case Study in Transformational Change," presents a major initiative that I led in the late 1980s. The work spanned six years and involved six large U.S. hospitals. This seminal work precipitated a major rethink of how patient care is organized and delivered, and evidence of it can be seen in most large hospitals today. It is without question the most significant and successful operational change initiative that I was part of during my career.

I hope that this three-part approach stimulates the thinking of today's change agents. Sections I and II describe various elements and approaches to the change agency process. Section III brings all these factors to bear in one game-changing transformational case study.

Finally, I need to comment on the relevance of my experience in change agency and the present-day usefulness of the examples cited herein. It is true that most of these case studies took place twenty to thirty years ago. My experience since then has confirmed the old adage: "The more things change, the more they stay the same." As I survey the business landscape today, I see the same problems, the same issues, and the same opportunities as I did thirty years ago. I believe that the case studies are as applicable today as they were when the work was initially completed. They are the how, where, and why a change agent affects change. Read on and see if you agree.

ABOUT THE NUMBERS

Change is driven by numbers. Every successful change initiative begins by either defining the problem to be solved or describing the condition to be managed. And adverbs and adjectives just don't cut it. Numbers are essential. "Our costs are too high," an executive might say. Too high relative to what? And what does "too high" really mean—5%? 15%? 25%? Each of these answers could be true and the remedy for each would likely be very different.

The successful change agent must have a complete analytical tool kit to quantify and define issues, problems, and opportunities. "Wise men never argue about facts," my partner Tom Jones used to say. And such agreement requires the precision that only numbers can provide. Situations need to be defined objectively, not subjectively, if they are to be actionable.

All the examples provided in the chapters that follow were grounded in an analytical framework and loads of numbers. Some of the numbers I used in the examples are my best recollection of them at the time we did the work. Some I researched or talked over with former colleagues. To qualify each of these historical references would be cumbersome and would make for difficult reading. Therefore, I've simply used my best judgment to reconstruct the numbers. Some of them are precise. Some are accurate. Some are simplified and exaggerated to make a point. But all of them are representative and directionally correct.

ABOUT THE WORDS

This is a book written by a business person for business people. As such, much of the terminology should be familiar to you. That said, I am sure that some of you will not understand various words or phrases that are unique to change agents, and who knows, maybe even unique to me. This short glossary might help you along the way.

Billability: The percentage of a professional service worker's time that is devoted to work that can be charged to a client. See also: *Utilization*.

Goad: Someone who incites or prods. A stick with a pointed or electrically charged end for driving cattle.

Inventory Turns: The number of times inventory is sold or used in a given time period, usually a year. The equation for inventory turnover equals the cost of net sales divided by the average inventory.

Lateral Thinking: The solving of problems by an indirect and creative approach, typically by viewing the problem in a new and unusual light.

Lead Time: The time between the initiation and completion of a process, or a series of processes.

Monetize: To convert into money.

Price Elasticity: A measure used in economics to show the impact of the demand for a good or service in response to a change in its price.

Process: A systematic series of actions directed to some end.

SKU: A unique product identification code that helps track the item for inventory.

Utilization: The proportion of the available time, expressed as a percentage, that an employee, a piece of equipment, or a system is productively engaged.

Value-Added: The difference between the total revenues of a company and its total purchases from other companies.

Value Proposition: A company's reason for being: The products or services they provide, the customers they serve, and how they create tangible value for these customers.

Most of the technical terms I use in the book, including the ones noted above, I define in more detail in later chapters. I've included them here because you might stumble on them before the more detailed explanations.

THE CHANGE AGENT'S LAMENT

In the beginning was the Plan.
And then came the Assumptions.
And the Plan was without substance.
And the Assumptions were without reason.
And darkness was upon the face of the Workers.
And they spoke among themselves saying,
"This is a crock of shite and it stinks."

And the workers went unto their Supervisors and said,
"It is a pail of dung, and none may abide the odour thereof."
And the Supervisors went unto their Managers, saying,
"It is a smelly bucket of excrement, and none may abide it."
And the Managers went unto their Directors, saying,
"It is a vessel of fertilizer, and none may abide its strength."
And the Directors spoke among themselves saying to one another,
"It contains that which aids plant growth, and it is very strong."

And the Directors went to the Vice-Presidents, saying unto them,
"It promotes growth, and it is robust."
And the Vice-Presidents went unto the President, saying unto him,
"This new Plan will promote the growth and vigour of the company."
And the President looked upon the Plan and saw that it was good.
And then the Plan became Policy.
And that is how shit happens.

Source Unknown

THE CHANGE AGENT'S HANDBOOK

It is not the strongest of the species, nor the most intelligent, who will survive, but the one most responsive to change.
—LEON MEGGINSON

"hange is inevitable. Change is constant," Benjamin Disraeli once said. This statement is true in the personal and social aspects of our lives. But it is particularly true in our work lives. Companies and organizations are always changing: they change big and small things and all manner of things in between. Most people on the receiving end of change find this hard to accept. In most businesses, people like things the way they are. They personally don't want to make changes or be in the midst of change. They know what they must do and are comfortable with the status quo. This is not surprising. As my colleague Ferry de Bakker once said, "It's the warm comfort of routine."

Motivating people to embrace change can be a tough task. Offering facts and analysis of the situation as a justification for change may seem helpful, but it is rarely enough to cause people to change their ways. Just today, I read the following in the New York Times regarding the 2017 French presidential election: "The paradox of France is that it is desperate for reform—and desperate not to be reformed. It wants the benefits of a job-producing competitive economy but fears relinquishing a job-protecting uncompetitive one. A Macron presidency will have to devote its intellectual and rhetorical energies to explaining that it can be one or the other, but not both."[1]

New situations "can either generate personal growth or create personal fears. Which of these dominates is completely dependent upon how we view change. Change can be viewed as either exciting or frightening, but regardless of how we view it, we must all face the fact that change is the

---

1 Bret Stephens, "What Has Failed in France," *The New York Times*, May 5, 2017, www.nytimes.com/2017/05/05/opinion/what-has-failed-in-france.html.

very nature of life."[2]

Change agents tend to be those who view change as exciting. They thrive on leading the change process: defining the problem, developing the solution, persuading others to accept it, and guiding the implementation. They find gratification in seeing things improve. They like resolving the ambiguity inherent in any problematic situation, and articulating a new approach with clarity and purpose. And a crucial part of any change agent's job is getting those who view change as threatening to accept it. This almost always involves an emotional connection: addressing pain, fear, frustration, or insecurity. To convince anyone to adopt and sustain change, a change agent must be mindful of these four emotions. The Roman consul Cicero once said, "If you wish to persuade me, you must think my thoughts, feel my feelings, and speak my words."

This section offers six imperatives embodied by every successful change agent I know. They come from both my personal experience—successes and failures—and my observations of leaders, managers, and companies over the years. Some may find a few of these imperatives obvious, but it has always surprised me to see just how often they are not followed.

Each imperative is followed by two or three case-study examples drawn from my many years of leading change. The examples will provide some substance to the coaching points, and will take them out of the theoretical and into the real world.

These examples are applicable to a variety of organizations. Most of them came from large manufacturing and service-based companies. But they apply just as much to small start-up ventures, not-for-profit organizations, and community or civic associations.

And they work for all kinds of change agents, too: external folks like management consultants and executive coaches, as well as many "insiders"—managers, project leaders, IT professionals, finance staff—anyone who gets involved in leading change initiatives.

Most of these examples reveal two important patterns. First, sustainable change requires clearly defining the problem, coming up with a creative solution, and putting effective communications strategies in place. Second, you can't manage your way through a major change initiative without effective leadership. To be an effective leader, you must be aware of

---

[2] Michael A. Singer, *The Untethered Soul* (Oakland, CA: New Harbinger Publications, 2007), 71.

people's concerns and competing interests to get buy-in to a new approach. Change can be challenging, but without leadership, no positive change is possible.

CHAPTER 1

BUILD DISCIPLES

The greatest leader is not necessarily the one who does the greatest things. He is the one that gets the people to do the greatest things.
—RONALD REAGAN

Effective change agents never operate alone. They always work in teams of some sort: outside consulting teams, internal project teams, or ad hoc working groups. It's always a team. One person will never have adequate knowledge, experience, or influence to define a major problem and formulate its solution in isolation. It always requires teammates, or as I call them, *disciples*.

Your teammates should themselves be effective change agents, and as such, should almost always demonstrate a set of common characteristics to show that:

1. *They are smart.* They are quick thinkers. They can adapt their experience to new situations. They are logical. They can clearly articulate their thoughts and ideas. They are intellectually curious.

2. *They are mentally agile.* They often use analogies to prompt creative ideas. When working on unfamiliar problems or in new industries, analogies are often the easiest way to think about a new situation.

3. *They are analytical.* They use numbers to define problems and design solutions. They appreciate that adjectives, adverbs, and arm-waving lack the precision required to effectively define and solve a problem.

4. *They are self-confident.* They are not afraid to challenge authority or precedent. They may be introverted, they may be soft-spoken, but they are never meek. They speak their mind. They don't get bothered when others disagree.

5. *They have integrity.* They are honest. They speak truth to power, even when it is difficult or consequential. They have no hidden agendas. They always play their cards face-up and go wherever the facts take them.

Two keys to building a strong team of disciples are to (1) consistently hire talented people who exhibit the characteristics just described, and (2) develop them in a way that allows them to realize their full potential.

GET BEYOND THE RESUME

Recruiting is the starting point for building an effective team of change agents. And the most crucial step in recruiting is the interviewing process. Unfortunately, my experience is that the basis of most interviews is the candidate's resume. A typical interview goes something like this:

Interviewer: "I see that you spent three years as a Warehouse Supervisor at the Acme Company."

Candidate: "Yes I did."

Interviewer: "Tell me about that."

Candidate: "Well, I ran the warehouse. I had two supervisors and twenty hourly workers reporting to me, and we were responsible for receiving all incoming inventory and shipping all outgoing orders."

Interviewer: "Sounds challenging. How did you get offered the job in the first place?"

Candidate: "I had been the Shipping Supervisor for two years, and when the Warehouse Manager was fired, they offered me his job."

Interviewer: "Why did he get fired?"

Candidate: "He got accused of sexual harassment, and they found some e-mails that proved it."

Interviewer: "Ouch! So, what was your biggest accomplishment as Warehouse Manager?"

Candidate: "I was able to improve on time delivery performance by 15% while simultaneously reducing labor costs by 8%."

✳

You get the idea. The interviewer learned virtually nothing about the candidate that couldn't have been gleaned from his resume. There was no need to rehash it. And yet that is what most interviewers do. That doesn't help them to learn if the candidate is smart, a quick thinker, facile with analogies, or articulate. Such an interview would have been a non-starter at Booz Allen.

The success of major management consulting firms is, quite literally, driven by their people. They don't make products. They don't really provide services, at least not in the same sense that an architect or a CPA does. Instead, they try to help their clients solve problems or exploit opportunities. As one colleague suggested, "We're just brains on a stick." Now I'm not sure that I'd go quite that far, but a good management consultant is usually pretty cerebral.

Thus, recruiting was perhaps the most important and strategic thing that we did. Many partners and staff at Booz Allen played an active role in recruiting. I was one of those folks. I maintained close ties to the faculty at my alma mater, Carnegie Mellon University, so I could identify the stars in each new MBA class. I gave presentations about the firm at CMU and other business schools every year. I did on-campus interviews. And I did office interviews.

At Booz Allen, each candidate would be subjected to one of two types of interview. These were split evenly and decided in advance. One was an achievement screen: Where has the candidate been successful in the past? What do they aspire to do? Are they articulate? Have they demonstrated leadership potential? Do they get rattled easily?

The other was an analytical screen: How smart is the candidate? How do they approach problem-solving? Can they break a problem down into its parts? Do they try to dimension things with numbers? Are they logical? Do they use analogies?

I had one candidate tell me, many years after the fact, that his on-campus Booz Allen interview was "the most difficult two hours of my life." I don't know if they were that bad. But they were tough, and they were rigorous.

One tool that I used frequently in analytical screens was the One-Minute Mystery. I would give the candidate a situation and tell them to ask me whatever questions they wanted to try to figure out the mystery. Here is a simple example to give you an idea of how it worked:

Me: A man's very short conversation cost him a quarter, but he wasn't using a pay phone. Explain.

Candidate: Did he pay someone to borrow their phone?

Me: No.

Candidate: Does a phone have anything to do with the answer?

Me: No.

Candidate: Did the man buy something with the quarter?

Me: No.

Candidate: Hmmm. You said it was a short conversation. Was it longer than a minute?

Me: No.

Candidate: Does the conversation have anything to do with the answer?

Me: Yes.

Candidate: Was the man happy?

Me: No.

Candidate: Was he angry or upset?

Me: Yes.

Candidate: Is this what the conversation was about?

Me: Yes.

Candidate: Was the quarter a coin?

Me: No.

Candidate: Was it a time period?

Me: Yes.

Candidate: Was the man an athlete?

Me: Yes.

Candidate: Did this also involve the referee?

Me: Yes.

Candidate: Did someone get thrown out of a game?

Me: Yes. The basketball player cussed out the ref at the end of the third quarter and got thrown out of the game, thus costing him the fourth quarter.

This is a somewhat simplistic example. But you get the idea. The point of these exercises was not to see if the candidate could get the right answer. In this example, if the candidate had known the story and given the right answer immediately, I would have learned nothing. What these exercises allowed me to do was to get inside the head of the interviewee and take a peek at their wiring: Are they smart? Are they mentally agile? Are they analytical? Are they articulate? Are they self-confident? Are they telling you what they think or what they think you want to hear?

The achievement screen was entirely different. We explored leadership roles that the candidate had held, often in non-work related, extracurricular activities, like sports team captaincies or student government; places where their leadership role was earned by the trust and respect of their peers. Often these roles did not appear on their resume.

I also explored their intellectual curiosity by throwing out random questions and seeing how they engaged with them. And of course, I gave them the Pittsburgh airport test: "Could you handle being stranded in the Pittsburgh airport with this person for eight hours during a snow storm, or would you have to slit your wrists?"

Finally, I would often ask candidates off-the-wall questions to see if they were mentally agile and clever. Here are two questions that I used to use, followed by some actual winning and losing answers:

Me: How do I tie my shoes?

Candidate #1: You take the laces, cross them, and make a knot. (Sorry, Charlie: no offer.)

Candidate #2: It's easy. You score exactly as many points as your shoes scored. That way you're tied. (He got an offer, and he took it.)

✳

Me: Have you ever done time in prison?

Candidate #1: Absolutely not. That question was offensive. (He didn't get an offer.)

Candidate #2: Does one night in jail for a drunk and disorderly count? (She got an offer, accepted it, and was elected to the partnership six years later.)

✳

Your job as an interviewer is to figure out how the candidate is wired, both intellectually and emotionally. You need to separate the contenders from the pretenders. And you will rarely learn this by simply discussing the highlights of their resume.

MIND YOUR ABCs

Once you have hired talented people, you need to develop them. Everybody has heard the term "A-player." It describes the ultimate worker, colleague, or teammate. Their work, or play, as may be the case, is consistently outstanding. They are self-starters. They always go the extra mile. They never need to be told something twice. They are natural thought leaders.

But there are also B-players who fall short of the ideal in some dimensions. Maybe they are not as quick-minded. Maybe they tend to miss deadlines. Maybe they are a tad disorganized. They are contributors, and their performance adds value. But they are just not in the A-player's league.

Then there are the C-players. They consistently fall short of standards and expectations. They rarely make meaningful contributions. They are not really engaged. They often seem to have their own agenda. Their personality does not fit with the group. They often miss deadlines. They are clearly a hiring mistake. Those who interviewed them probably just talked them through their resume.

So, what to do? I worked with a number of colleagues who were outstanding managers and leaders, but only when dealing with A-players. They were seemingly intolerant of anyone else. They would berate and humiliate them. One went on to become the COO of a Fortune 100 company and was in line to succeed the CEO when he retired. When that day came, however, he was denied the CEO position by the board of directors because he was always so judgmental and organizationally disruptive. He couldn't build a team.

Given a normal distribution of employees, 15% will be As. 70% will be Bs. And 15% will be Cs. It's a law of nature. You can look it up. That means that you must get value out of your B-players if you have any hope of succeeding. The quest for more and more A-players will never pan out.

Sam Walton reportedly said that he had simply built a company where average people could perform like stars. That means he created a system of policies, processes, authorities, empowerment, and information that enabled 85% of his employees to perform at very high levels relative to expectations. Wal-Mart's success was not an accident.

In my experience, you need to manage As, Bs, and Cs very differently. Start with the A-players. You must, I repeat *must*, do everything in your power to retain them. You must keep them challenged and allow them to grow. And you certainly must reward them. These are folks who routinely get job offers from other firms and companies.

Both when I was a global practice leader at Booz Allen and when I was Chief Financial Officer of Burson-Marsteller, 60% to 70% of annual staff compensation increases awarded by me would go to the A-players. The

Bs would get the rest, and the Cs would get nothing. That's right! Nothing! You simply can't risk losing an A-player because you didn't give her the largest raise possible, and instead rewarded, even slightly, a relative non-contributor.

Then, you must develop the B-players. These are capable people with much to offer if they are nurtured and guided. This is where good managers spend most of their time. You can send them to outside classes or give them materials to read. You can coach them and pull ideas out of them. You can have them watch you edit a letter or report they have written, while you verbally describe everything you are changing and why. I've personally done this many times with great effect. You have no choice but to invest in and develop B-players. There are simply not enough A-players to go around.

Finally, we come to the C-players. There are two types of C-player: the misplaced and the asshole. The misplaced person is simply in the wrong job. Try to find a position that suits their skills, but put a time limit on this effort. The asshole is just that. They have no clue that they aren't contributing. They often exhibit arrogance or an unfounded self-confidence that makes them even harder to tolerate. Make them disappear. Now!

You will never get either C-player to an acceptable level of performance and contribution without a disproportionate level of time and effort. And they will not be missed. In fact, the rest of your organization is keenly aware that these folks are not pulling their own weight. And they are watching you to see what you will do.

Do not try to rehabilitate C-players. Counsel them to find other work, and, if they have the right attitude, allow them to continue to work for thirty days while they try to secure another job. If they are likely to become disruptive, just show them the door. At Booz Allen, we force-ranked the entire client staff every year, and counseled out the bottom 15%.

A successful corporate goad needs to build a team of like-minded people who thrive on defining and solving problems. This chapter has offered two keys to this challenge. First, recruiting is paramount. And you need to get beyond superficial discussions if you are going to discover real talent. Second, once you have recruited talented teammates, you must develop them. Some merely require challenge and direction. Others require active, hands-on coaching. But develop you must.

You can act on these ideas immediately. The next time you are called to interview a candidate, review their resume in advance and set it to the side. Then put together a written guide to prompt you through the interview. Form questions, pose riddles, challenge conventional wisdom; anything to get inside the head of the candidate and help you determine if they are smart, mentally agile, analytical, self-confident, and honest.

As to development, start with an employee or a colleague who is currently on your team. Think through their demonstrated strengths and weaknesses. And then creatively prepare a plan for helping them to work on their development needs, and review it with them. Maybe they need to take a course in statistics. Maybe they need to practice giving a presentation. Maybe they need to write a report and have you thoroughly critique it. Whatever is required, proactively develop your team.

Finding, attracting, developing, rewarding, and retaining talent is key to building a set of disciples. This is the first step in leading and inspiring transformational change within and across any organization.

CHAPTER 2

LEAD FROM THE FRONT

If your actions inspire others to dream more, learn more,
do more and become more, you are a leader.
—DOLLY PARTON

Management is not leadership. "Management is a set of processes that can keep a complicated system of people and technology running smoothly. The most important aspects of management include planning, budgeting, organizing, staffing, controlling, and problem-solving. Leadership is a set of processes that creates organizations in the first place or adapts them to significantly changing circumstances. Leadership defines what the future should look like, aligns people with that vision, and inspires them to make it happen despite the obstacles."[3] A successful transformation is usually 80% leadership and only 20% management.

"Unfortunately for us today, this emphasis on management has been institutionalized in corporate cultures that discourage employees from learning how to lead. Ironically, past success is usually the key ingredient in producing this outcome. The syndrome, as I have observed it on many occasions, goes like this: Success creates some degree of market dominance, which in turn produces much growth. After a while, keeping the ever-larger organization under control becomes the primary challenge. Attention turns inward, and managerial competencies are nurtured. With a strong emphasis on management but not leadership, bureaucracy and an inward focus take over. But with continued success, the result mostly of market dominance, the problem often goes unaddressed and an unhealthy

---

[3] John P. Kotter, *Leading Change* (Boston: Harvard Business Review Press, 2012), 28.

arrogance begins to evolve. All of these characteristics then make transformative effort much more difficult."[4]

At the same time, "arrogant managers can overevaluate their current performance and competitive position, listen poorly, and learn slowly. Inwardly focused employees can have difficulty seeing the very forces that present threats and opportunities. Bureaucratic cultures can smother those who want to respond to changing conditions. And the lack of leadership leaves no force inside these organizations to break out of the morass."[5]

Change agents need to have a strong set of managerial competencies, including planning, scheduling, problem-solving, and project management. But at their core, they are not managers, they are leaders. They reject the status quo. They envision innovative ways of doing business. They are alert to competitive threats. They thrive on new opportunities. And they lead organizations and people to respond.

Leadership is both an action and a state of being. There is no permanence of position in being a leader. You lead for as long as the people believe in you and are willing to follow. Leaders are not necessarily those with the most important title or the most authority.[6] They are the ones with a following, and they almost always lead from the front, like the Calvary officer on a horse out in front of his troops.

GEL THE TEAM

One of the responsibilities of the managing partner of an office at Booz Allen Hamilton was to hold regular staff meetings. The partners and staff were routinely traveling all over the country, and at times, all over the world. Keeping everyone up to date with information about the firm and about each other was a major challenge.

When I took over as managing partner of the Atlanta office in the late 1980s, I decided that monthly staff meetings were too frequent, so I scheduled them quarterly. I also thought there should be an important social aspect to these events, so I held them offsite, started them at 4:00 p.m. on Fridays, and followed them with a cocktail hour, and at times, a voluntary dinner.

---

[4] Kotter, *Leading Change*, 30.

[5] Kotter, *Leading Change*, 31.

[6] Larry Taylor, *Be an Orange* (Houston: Orange Press, 1992), 95.

Staff meetings usually covered housekeeping items, such as new hires, promotions, anniversaries, and birthdays. I talked about the performance of the firm and about new, interesting client assignments that had recently been won. And I reviewed various new policies and programs.

Finally, I gave the staff a chance to bring up any issues or concerns or ideas that they wanted to discuss. At one meeting, our receptionist, Ginny, raised the subject of charitable giving.

"Does the firm support any charities or other outreach programs?" she asked.

"Yes," I said. "I don't know the firm-wide numbers, but last year the Atlanta office donated $25,000."

"Who decides where the money goes?" she continued.

"The partners generally decide what initiatives to support," I answered.

"Why do the partners get to decide?" she asked. "Shouldn't our charitable giving reflect the desires of the whole office, not just the views of a few partners?"

"Good idea," I responded. "Why don't you, Chris, and Coleen form a committee and brainstorm how our charitable giving ought to work, and then come back to all of us with a set of recommendations." As I said, Ginny was the office receptionist. Coleen was a secretary. And Chris was a senior associate on the client service staff. I knew that all three of them enjoyed the respect of their colleagues. And importantly, none of them was a partner.

At the next staff meeting, Ginny presented their recommendations: first, the entire office would elect a Contributions Committee of four people. Anyone was eligible. Then the committee would poll their colleagues, develop an overall giving strategy, and propose the initial recipients of our support. The initial budget would be $30,000 per year.

The staff was unanimously supportive of Ginny's proposal. In fact, she got a standing ovation and a few shout-outs that we should put her on the client staff. I called for an immediate election, and we located some pencils and paper.

"Vote for four of your colleagues to represent you on the newly formed Contributions Committee," I instructed, and everyone voted. After collecting the ballots, I asked one of my colleagues to tally the votes. He returned ten minutes later and announced the four winners. It was the original three folks—Ginny, Coleen, and Chris—plus our graphic designer, Peggy. Not a partner in sight.

Then Chris stood and said to his fellow committee members, "I propose that we elect Ginny as our chairman. She's the one that got this ball rolling."

Coleen and Peggy both said, "I vote yes," and Ginny was elected chairman. Just like that. This entire process took maybe thirty minutes. And for the thirty staff members in the meeting, it was an aspirational and inspirational half hour.

At the next staff meeting, Ginny presented their plan: we would give money only to causes that we were willing to support with our time; we would limit donations to two causes, so as to achieve maximum impact; and we would support one cause related to the arts and one that supported children. This, she said, represented the consensus view of the entire office.

She said that the committee had selected the Atlanta Symphony Young Artists program, wherein we would underwrite one weekend concert during the season that featured an up-and-coming classical musician. And we would get personally involved by hosting a reception for the artist and inviting several business and community leaders to meet with him or her. As an aside, our first artist was now-famed violinist Midori, who was only sixteen years old when she performed with the Atlanta Symphony Orchestra.

The second cause that the committee proposed was CURE Childhood Cancer. This organization funded research into childhood cancer and led the fight to find a cure. But more important to our folks was their patient and family services work. They ran something akin to a Ronald McDonald House that hosted family members when their children were in the hospital for treatment. They also had support groups to help the kids and their parents cope with this horrible disease.

In addition to our $15,000 per year in monetary support, the entire office really got involved with this organization. CURE offered us a seat on their board, and of course, we gave it to Ginny. Folks from the office baked cookies at least once a week for the kids and their parents. Each year, we hosted a big picnic at Stone Mountain for the kids, their parents, and their physicians and caregivers. By the third year, this picnic was nothing short of amazing. We got Coca-Cola to donate the use of one of their concession trailers and provide free soft drinks. We got other Atlanta-based companies to donate food and supplies. We got the Georgia Tech cheerleaders to make an appearance and put on a show. Some of our people dressed up as clowns. Some ran games for the kids. Others cooked burgers and hot dogs.

We probably served two hundred people that year.

For a lot of our staff, this was the most rewarding day of the year; it provided an opportunity to give back in a way that really mattered. On the other hand, for many, the day was also the toughest one of the year. Watching these children just broke your heart. Some showed up in ambulances and on gurneys and had to remain connected to their IVs during the picnic. Lots of them were bald because of the effects of their chemotherapy. But they were kids, and for one afternoon, they could forget about their problems and just have fun.

The involvement of the Atlanta office staff in these outreach events probably did more for morale and team-building than anything else that we did. They really brought the group together. And it's amazing to think that it all came out of a staff meeting where our receptionist, Ginny, simply asked, "Does the firm support any charities or other outreach programs?"

Team-building is not about rah-rah speeches or contrived exercises. True team-building occurs when the team takes on a purpose that binds its members together in an emotional way, be it a cause, a problem, or a passion. This is how you gel your team into a force bigger than its individual members.

DEVELOP ALLIES

My father was a manufacturing executive in a factory that had a powerful and aggressive union, and he was always complaining about them and their unreasonable demands. Later, in business school, there was a decidedly anti-union bias among the faculty and the students.

So, in my early days, I too was biased against unions. But my view changed over the next twenty years as I had the opportunity to work in union shop environments and involve union leaders in our day-to-day work. There are unreasonable and value-destroying unions to be sure. But my experience was that most unions were a real asset to their companies.

In a large operation with thousands of workers, a good union can and does play a vital role in employee communications. They also drive equity and fairness in employee relations, and can positively influence their members when change is introduced.

I also found most of the local union leaders to be smart and thoughtful. In fact, in many cases, I found them to be smarter than the management team and to care more about the sustainability of the company. These were some solid citizens and the companies were lucky to have them. Not all of them, but lots of them.

Over my career, I probably had five or six major assignments that required me to deal with a union at some level. But without question, the most significant one was the United Auto Workers Local 1268 in Belvidere, Illinois.

In 1980, I was part of a team that tried to bring Chrysler back from the brink of bankruptcy. We had initially been retained by them to analyze the business and support their application for $1.5 billion in loan guarantees from the federal government. We determined that they had a reasonable chance of turning the business around and avoiding the loss of perhaps 150,000 jobs.

Our Chairman, Jim Farley, and Chrysler CEO Lee Iacocca met with the Secretary of the Treasury, the Comptroller of Currency, and the Chairman of the Federal Reserve to discuss the matter. The group decided to proceed with the loan guarantee program, but required Chrysler to obtain an additional $2 billion in unguaranteed loans, which they did. The government also demanded that Chrysler retain Booz Allen to lead a major cost reduction and revenue enhancement initiative, and to report back to the feds periodically as to Chrysler's progress.

Carl Blonkvist, Dave Guza, Randy Myer, and I comprised the manufacturing team, and we did most of our work out of the Chrysler assembly plant in Belvidere, Illinois. This plant made the Dodge Omni and Plymouth Horizon, and employed around 6,000 people. We used this plant to discover, develop, and test opportunities to improve performance. If proven, these initiatives would be rolled out at other Chrysler factories around the world.

Randy tackled all the supply chain management issues and opportunities. I focused my attention on factory labor and assembly line efficiency. We jointly assessed the purchasing function in Detroit. This was time-critical work with a lot at stake. It was also a lot to wrap your arms—and your head—around.

My first week in Belvidere, I decided that I would clearly need the help and support of the union if we were going to make any significant reductions in labor costs and any improvements to assembly line efficiency. I met the local union president in the temporary office that we had been assigned, and proceeded to tell him why we were there: to find cost savings, to cut hundreds of jobs in order to save thousands of others, and to ultimately help Chrysler avoid bankruptcy and regain their viability.

When I was through, he said to me that he appreciated what we were trying to do and wished us Godspeed, but before he would agree to help, I would have to pass a test. He told me that there was a situation on the Trim I section of the assembly line: "There is a woman who has apparently been assigned the job of looking after two foremen. She is an hourly worker, but instead of being assigned to a station on the line, she spends her time talking to the foremen in their office, and only leaves to get them coffee and donuts, or to occasionally get their cars washed. This really pisses off the other assembly line workers."

Then he explained my test: "As soon as you can get this gal out of the office and back working on the line, I will happily help you in any way that I can." And he stood up and walked out.

I first went down to the Trim I line to confirm what I had been told. Sure enough, there was an attractive woman who was sitting in an office drinking coffee and talking to a foreman. I then went directly to the office of Herb Stone, the plant manager, and told him of my conversation with the union president and the apparent situation on the line. We then went out to Trim I so he could see things for himself. Sure enough, coffee and donuts!

When I arrived at the plant the next morning, I went directly to Trim I and was very happy to see the attractive blonde installing radios into vehicles as they moved past her. I went to my office and called the union president. He said that he would be right up.

He walked in the office and shook my hand. "Congratulations! I'm sure you know that Phyllis is back on the line, but you may not know that both foremen have been fired. You passed the test. Now what can I do to help?"

For the next several months, he and I worked closely together. He was a smart and creative man, and was full of promising ideas. Often when I presented a novel approach, he would say: "That way won't work. But if you do it this way, I think that it will."

One time he explained to me why and how he reacted to my various proposals. "My job," he said, "is to try to make things fair and equitable for my members. No one objects to working hard, as long as it is equitable."

He then asked me about the current line balance efficiency. Think of this as how many productive minutes the average line worker works in an hour. 90% would mean that in any given hour, the average line worker would be working for fifty-four minutes and idle for six minutes.

"93%," I responded.

"Well," he said, "I'd be happy to see that improve to 97%, as long as every worker's efficiency was somewhere between 95% and 99%. That is equitable and I can sell it to my members. Where I get in trouble is when some workers are at 75% while others are at 110%. I can't sell that to my members because it's just not fair."

We made lots of progress at the Belvidere Assembly Plant, thanks in large part to the cooperation of the union. As I remember, we reduced labor costs by 5%, which is a very big deal in the auto industry. Similar improvements were implemented throughout the company.

By building a strong relationship with the local union president based on mutual trust and a shared mission, we were able to lead the change process together and achieve buy-in from the rank-and-file workers. Undoubtedly, this could not have been achieved absent our relationship.

Chrysler righted the ship pretty quickly. In addition to basic cost reduction and revenue enhancement, they introduced the new K-cars: Aries, Reliant, and LeBaron. All of this enabled them to repay the $3.5 billion in loans in less than three years.

PUT YOURSELF OUT THERE

Without question, my craziest staff meeting ever took place on Friday, October 13, 1989, four days after my fortieth birthday. We held the meeting and the subsequent reception at the Ritz-Carlton hotel in downtown Atlanta, just a block from our office. The staff meeting turned a little ugly as I had to announce a new policy that pretty much ticked off the entire client service staff.

One of the perks of working at Booz Allen had been a long-standing policy of being allowed to fly first class. The client staff appreciated this benefit very much because most of them took several flights every week. For example, at one point, I was Delta Airlines' twenty-third best customer in the world.

But it seems that the managing partner of the U.S. business thought we could save some money by changing the first-class air policy and requiring everyone to fly coach. And he had the support of most of the New York partners, one of whom told me, "I rarely fly. The change doesn't affect me at all. And maybe I'll make a little more money!"

When I presented this new policy to the staff, they were angry. They threatened to hide their first-class upgrade fees somewhere in their expense reports. It took me a long time to calm them down and suggest that they didn't want to lose their integrity and risk losing their jobs over a stupid policy change.

At that time, Delta Airlines offered their frequent flyers first-class upgrades for $10, $20, or $30, depending on the duration of the flight. "Just pay for the upgrade yourself and don't worry about it," I counseled them. "It's just not a big deal. And if you can't afford the thirty bucks, come see me, and I'll give it to you out of my own pocket." That seemed to quiet them down.

We adjourned the meeting and moved on to the reception. I thought as we walked into the room that the staff needed a little bit of a blowout to get them out of their first-class funk. And boy did they get one.

I knew that several of my partners from other offices had been invited to the reception, as there was a plan to celebrate my fortieth birthday. I had begged my partner, Gary Shows, not to do anything crazy or embarrassing, and told him that I just wanted to share a few drinks with my colleagues.

Things were going smoothly and I was into my third drink when I heard a commotion at the door. Into the room marched this big-chested, small-waisted blonde in a nurse's uniform that was about two sizes too small. And then she started coming my way. The staff could already smell blood.

She walked directly up to me and said, "Kurt, I'm Nurse Goodbody, here to give you your fortieth birthday physical exam. Please take off your clothes."

Now at this point, lots of thoughts went through my head. If I did nothing, I was going to be the brunt of fifteen minutes of sick and embarrassing humor. On the other hand, I was the managing partner of the office; I couldn't take off my clothes. But I had decided earlier that the staff needed a blowout tonight, hadn't I? What the hell, I thought, you only live once.

I set my drink down and slowly began to remove my clothes: first, my tie; then my shoes and socks; then my shirt; then, after pausing to reconsider, my slacks; then my undershirt. I was now down to my tighty-whities.

The staff was going nuts, hooting and hollering and cheering me on. At that point, I decided that I had gone far enough. I was not going full commando in front of the staff. So I sat down in a chair and said, "I'm ready, Nurse Goodbody."

Before I continue with the story, I must admit to being confused about people's reaction to underwear. I've had this confusion for as long as I can remember. Most people seem to be relaxed and comfortable around other people wearing bathing suits, but people tend to freak out when they see folks in their undies. Are boxers all that different from swimming trunks? How is a bikini different than a bra and panties? I'm as comfortable showing myself in my underwear as I am in my bathing suit. I guess that I'm just weird that way.

Back to Nurse Goodbody: She leaned over me, pretending to listen to my heart with her stethoscope, and whispered in my ear, "I've been doing this act for three years, and no one has ever taken their clothes off. I don't know what to do."

I whispered back, "Well, you had better figure it out because you're the one who is going to be embarrassed if you can't come up with something." Her "exam" continued and the staff went crazy, cheering both of us on. All thought of the new airfare policy magically disappeared.

Sometimes leadership requires that you put yourself out there and do something outrageous and unexpected. This can often move your team beyond their issues, problems, and frustrations by serving as a pressure release valve.

There are lots of ways to lead a team. A problem or a situation may provide the basis on which the team is formed, but teamwork is rooted in shared experiences. The first and last case studies in this chapter provided two excellent examples of leading such team-building experiences. The Contributions Committee brought the partners and staff together around a common cause. And the work we did with CURE created a strong emotional bond among and across the staff. The Nurse Goodbody performance once again provided a shared experience, albeit one rooted in humor and stress relief. The staff bonded around my embarrassment.

In the case of the Chrysler example, the local UAW president and I were a two-man team. We gelled by virtue of a demonstrated commitment to substantively deal with the issues, and not allow politics or the powers-that-be to hijack the process. Again, it was the shared experience of getting Phyllis back to work that sealed the deal.

Often, your allies are not the people you would expect. Union leaders or management folks, sure; but they also might be auditors, or regulators, or even tax authorities. Stay open-minded about forging alliances.

To accomplish important things, you always need colleagues and allies by your side. Talent is a must, but your people will not provide real value unless they are led and gelled into a team. And you're the one who must do it.

CHAPTER 3

GET THEIR ATTENTION

The best leaders inspire by example. When that's not an option, brute intimidation works pretty well, too.
—Larry Kersten

Most people are reluctant to change. It doesn't matter what the change is, they don't want to do it. Change is threatening. Change is scary. Change is demanding work. This is as true for changing personal lifestyles and behaviors at home as it is for changing business strategies, processes, policies, or reporting relationships at work. To be successful, change agents need to start by getting the attention of those impacted by the change: those who must embrace the change for it to happen, and those who will be forced to work differently in the future.

As John Kotter has pointed out, reluctance to change is, at its core, driven by complacency. This, in turn, is supported by the very human tendency to deny that which we do not want to hear. Life is usually more pleasurable without problems and more difficult with them. Most of us, most of the time, think we have enough challenges to keep us busy. We're not looking for more work. So, when evidence of a big problem appears, if we can get away with ignoring the information, we often will.[7]

As Dr. Kotter says, "Never underestimate the magnitude of the forces that reinforce complacency and help to maintain the status quo."[8] There are times when you simply must get the attention of the organization if you are going to get them to change.

---

[7] Kotter, *Leading Change*, 44.
[8] Kotter, *Leading Change*, 44.

THIS IS NOT A DEBATING SOCIETY

Booz Allen was a very collegial place. Partners and staff got on well. We played well with each other. We socialized. We learned from our failures. And we shared in our successes. That said, there was a level of discipline governing our behavior and our adherence to policies that was usually accepted and rarely challenged.

The percentage of our time spent on work that could be billed to clients (billability) was the primary driver of the firm's operating margins and profitability. We all did our best to help achieve and exceed our individual billability targets. Most completed time sheets and expense reports on time. Partners generally managed their accounts receivable and pressured clients to pay in a timely manner.

Other firms, however, allowed the culture of collegiality to erode discipline in key areas of personal responsibility: partners not sending timely invoices, client staff accepting and even encouraging low billability, staff ignoring the need for time and expense reporting for weeks at a time.

This lack of discipline, and the business cultures that tolerated it, carried over into other areas, such as accepting and adhering to new policies and processes that were part of a major change initiative. Too many folks held to the view that consensus was required before any change could be implemented, and they passively refused to participate until such consensus was achieved. This was collegiality gone awry.

The poster child for such a culture had to have been Burson-Marsteller, the world's largest public relations and marketing communications firm back in 1993 when I began to work with them. The then-CEO, Larry Snoddon, retained me to take a critical look at their business and recommend several ways to improve their performance.

At that time, Burson was a $300 million business with seventy-five offices in forty-five countries. Their work was focused on large, global companies, although they had lots of small-dollar clients, or cats and dogs as I called them. I discovered early in the work that they did not effectively measure or manage the utilization (billability) of their client staff, even though this was the primary driver of their profitability. No surprise, their profit margin was something like 2% globally.

I pulled together the data to allow me to determine the billable hours of the U.S. staff from the previous year. They had charged clients for only 48% of their available time! It was no wonder they didn't make any money. The other 52% of their time, they were prospecting for new clients, working on internal projects, attending training sessions, attending conferences, or just plain idle.

From my experience in professional service firms, they should have been able to achieve an 80% utilization rate, which would have driven profit margins above 30%. At Booz Allen, we routinely achieved 85% client staff billability.

I also found that client invoicing and collections processes were out of control. They had very large unbilled client charges, and their open accounts receivable averaged over one hundred and twenty days. By contrast, at Booz Allen, receivables were usually between thirty and forty days. This implied that Burson had over $100 million tied up in unnecessary working capital to fund these receivables.

There were other examples of expensive problems caused by the processes, policies, systems, and culture of the firm. It took them fifty days to close the books each month. Yes, managers got March financial results near the end of May. And client-sensitive information was haphazardly stored, and access to it was not controlled. I should point out that the Burson management team was not composed of stupid people. These were smart and capable professionals. It was just that they failed to measure and monitor key performance metrics.

Larry and I, and his senior management team, set about trying to fix things. We made substantial progress in making better information available to management on a timelier basis so they could begin to address many of these issues.

We were less successful in getting their attention and getting them to manage in a different way. We made progress, but it was slow going. Consistent with their culture, Larry kept trying to persuade instead of demand. I counseled him to fire a few of the poorer performers to get the attention of the organization. But he, too, resisted making dramatic changes. As a result, their financial performance continued to be poor and was unacceptable to Young & Rubicam.

In 1994, Larry was moved to a Y&R corporate position, and Tom Bell took over as CEO. My work with Burson not only continued; it ramped up. Tom had run the Washington, D.C. office of Burson, and had been part of the senior management team that was implementing the performance improvement initiatives I had been championing. He was one of the few who not only got it, but acted on it. He wanted me to continue to serve as a change agent and to try to speed the implementation process.

Tom also had another issue: he was concerned that the firm's overall value proposition was outdated, and that Burson had become a tactical, low-margin, commodity provider of public relations and marketing communications services. This means that their service offerings were transactional in nature and were offered by virtually all other competitors at a commodity price. Writing a simple press release for a client announcing their new product would be a good example of this.

Tom and I began to work together on another initiative: this one to create, develop, and implement a new value proposition that would position the firm as a strategic, high-margin, differentiated partner to their clients.

During Tom's first few months as CEO, we developed a new service offering called *perception management*, which held that the customer's perception of a client's product or service was usually more important than the reality, and that those perceptions could be created and reinforced through a time-tested methodology. Tom tried this new offering with several of his own clients, and they found it to be compelling and potentially valuable. For Burson, it was strategic, high-margin, and competitively differentiated.

We began to roll this out within the organization in a thoughtful and measured way. While we did see some success, most senior practitioners refused to embrace it and wanted to argue for some other approach to improving the business. This went on for a few months. Tom grew increasingly frustrated with the organization's slowness in changing its basic business practices and its refusal to embrace perception management.

Tom's frustration came to a head about five months after he had taken over as CEO. He called a meeting of the entire European management team in Venice, Italy. There were probably forty senior managers present from regional headquarters and the twenty or so European offices. I was also invited to attend and participate in the two-day meeting.

At the start of the meeting, the country manager of Italy welcomed all her colleagues and then introduced Tom Bell. Tom stood, walked to the podium, and turned to face the audience. The very first words out of his mouth were: "This is not a debating society! Fuck consensus! We are doing things my way!"

I won't claim that Tom's comments had an immediate and lasting impact. But they sure got the attention of everyone in the room. And it wasn't long before they were known to every manager in every office around the world. There was a new man in charge. And things were going to change. It appeared that Tom had all of the makings of a true corporate goad.

We continued to make progress, but it was still tough sledding. Then in 1997, at Tom's insistence, Young & Rubicam bought our consulting firm. Three months later, I was asked to become Chief Financial Officer of Burson-Marsteller, reporting directly to Tom.

The rate of change increased with my newfound authority. We went to work on client staff utilization and receivables management, and over the next two years, U.S. profit margins increased from 11% to 28%. Worldwide margins increased to 12%. Receivables were reduced from one hundred and twenty days to fifty. And the time it took to close the books each month was reduced from fifty days to six. Perception management continued to define our value proposition, but it never really got traction with most of the client leaders.

In 1999, Tom left Burson to become CEO of Young & Rubicam, and we sold the agency to WPP Group in 2000 for $4.7 billion. I'm sure that many of the improvements we initiated remain in place today. But absent its thought-leader, Tom Bell, perception management didn't get traction. In my experience, it can take several years to effectively change a culture. We just ran out of time and champions.

CHEAP THEATRICS

My first job out of college was in Production & Inventory Control with Industrial Nucleonics Corporation in Columbus, Ohio. For me, the greatest thing about the company was that they were very progressive and willing to invest time and money in the latest management and technology developments. The field of production and inventory control was undergoing a massive transformation enabled by the increasing availability and power of the computer. IBM developed one of the first, most comprehensive, and most integrated production planning systems—COPICS (Communications Oriented Production Information and Control System)—and Industrial Nucleonics was a beta test site for its development. The company was truly at the leading edge of this functional transformation.

I began in 1971 as an Expediter, and my job was to hustle up parts so that customer systems and sub-systems could be assembled, tested, and shipped. In 1972, I was promoted to Material Control Supervisor, and among other duties, I was responsible for the stockroom.

One of the absolute requirements of an integrated production planning system like COPICS is inventory record accuracy. Accurate on-hand balances are critical to calculating time-phased material requirements out into the future. And the stakes are higher when the component demands are highly interdependent: i.e., when the demand for one component is a function of the demand for a higher-level subassembly, which in turn is a function of a yet higher-level subassembly. The demand at each level of this hierarchy is first fulfilled by the on-hand inventory of each component or subassembly. Thus, any inventory record errors have a cascading effect on planning.

In short, inventory record accuracy is a big deal. And in the 1970s, it was a problem that had not yet been confronted by most manufacturing companies.

The first requirement of the new control environment was to secure physical control of the inventory, and a caged and locked stockroom was the only way to accomplish this. At Industrial Nucleonics, we already had a caged stockroom with limited access. I just had to put locks on the doors and control the keys. This was a big change for a Manufacturing Department that was used to walking into the stockroom to get whatever they needed.

The next step was to restrict access to the stockroom. I prohibited anyone from entering except the employees who worked there. As the manager, I could enter. The supervisor, Arlene Felger, could enter. And all the hourly employees could, of course, enter. Everyone else was banned. I remember once when our Vice President of Manufacturing, Walt Cantor, let himself into the stockroom. Arlene read him the riot act and tossed him out. He was really pissed and came directly to me. "Good for Arlene," I replied when he told me what she had said and done. "We'll have to give her a raise."

Finally, we had to demand that any request for materials from the stockroom be accompanied by a requisition form. No paperwork, no parts. The stockroom workers had to learn that no excuses or promises to be back with the paperwork were acceptable. Period.

After we implemented these changes, we saw a marked improvement in inventory record accuracy. We traced the remaining errors back to basic sloppiness on the part of stockroom employees. They would put parts in the wrong bin or miscount receipts. Stupid little mistakes that added up over time.

I decided that I needed to get their attention. I went to the Engineering Department and had them create a new part number. 15768-001 was an Eisenhower silver dollar. And its specification sheet called for a silver dollar comprised of 8.33% nickel and 91.67% copper that was 38.1 mm in diameter, and so on.

I then went to the Purchasing Department and had them issue a purchase order for one hundred silver dollars (part number 15768-001) to the bank down the street. I went to Accounting and got a check for $100 referencing the new purchase order.

The next day, I went to the bank and met with the manager. I gave him the check and the purchase order and asked if he could box up one hundred silver dollars and deliver them in an hour, with a copy of the purchase order, to the receiving dock at Industrial Nucleonics. He readily agreed. Then I sat back to see what would happen.

Slightly before the scheduled delivery time, I went out to the receiving dock and hid behind a pillar. A bank employee brought the box in and gave it to a receiving clerk, who signed for it and carried it to a bench. When she opened the box, you would think that she had discovered the crown jewels. She counted the silver dollars very slowly. Then she counted them again.

I moved around so that I would still have a vantage point to observe the goings-on. When the receiving clerk delivered the coins to the stockroom, the same thing happened. The stock clerk acted like he was handling fine china. He counted the coins twice and then labeled a box, put them in it, and carefully put the box on a shelf in part number sequence.

The next morning, I called a meeting of all receiving and stockroom employees. I told them I had heard that Engineering had decided to incorporate a silver dollar into the design of a particular electronic subassembly due to its conductance properties and size. I said I had heard that we'd received a shipment of one hundred silver dollars the day before.

Then I said to them: "Now look. If you are going to screw up anything in the stockroom—miscounts, misplacements, paperwork errors, whatever—please, please let it be these silver dollars. They are the cheapest thing we have in inventory!" Then I left the room.

I was told that I got their attention. And our inventory record accuracy eventually improved to 99.8%.

✳

As I said at the beginning of this chapter, most people are reluctant to change. It doesn't matter what the change is, they don't want to do it. To be successful, change agents need to start by getting the attention of those impacted by the change: those who must embrace the change for it to happen, and those who will be forced to work differently once it does.

The way you choose to get their attention will depend greatly on your personality. If you are by nature introverted and soft-spoken, it would be out of character for you to do something outrageous. Instead, try something clever or otherwise engaging. If you are more of an extrovert, you can try something more dramatic and theatrical. Either way, you need to make it memorable.

And don't forget to appeal to their emotions. To get people to accept change, you must address their fear, frustration, or insecurity. This does not mean that you must build consensus. Nor must you temper your aggressiveness. You simply must be mindful of people's emotional reactions to proposed changes and offer them some sort of reassurance.

Either before or during the implementation of a major change initiative, there will come a time when you need to get the attention of the players. Be sincere. Be creative. Make it memorable. Be a goad!

CHAPTER 4

DEFINE THE PROBLEM

If I had an hour to solve a problem, I'd spend fifty-five minutes thinking about the problem and five minutes thinking about solutions.
—ALBERT EINSTEIN

The greatest challenge to any thinker is stating the problem in a way that will allow a solution.
—BERTRAND RUSSELL

The most important thing that a change agent does is to define the problem: clearly, unambiguously, and factually. I estimate that in 70% of the management consulting assignments I led, the client had initially defined the problem incorrectly.

There were many reasons for this. Some were trying to deal with symptoms of the problem, not the problem itself. Some had shaky data or no data at all. They just adopted any old convenient problem and went straight to the solution. Other times, the real problem was masked by faulty or incomplete analysis.

Randy Wayne White may have summed it up best in one of his Doc Ford novels: "Snatching at a conclusion in advance of data is a dangerous shortcut."

DEVELOP CONTEXT

Le Creuset is a French manufacturer best known for its colorfully-enameled cast-iron cookware, whose signature color is flame orange. They've been around since 1925. I'm sure that you have seen or used their pots and pans and Dutch ovens at some point. Today they produce all their enameled cookware in France, but in the 1980s, they split their production between their plants in Fresnoy-le-Grand, France, and Early Branch, South Carolina.

I received a call from their U.S. CEO, who said that he needed some help with his distribution function. I flew to South Carolina and met him in his office, where he described the company and told me about his issues with distribution.

Le Creuset divided cookware production between their two found-ries based on the prevailing foreign exchange rates between the U.S. and France. They employed a complicated manufacturing and finishing process that was largely manual to achieve the high quality of their cookware—so high that they offered a lifetime warranty on all Le Creuset cookware.

In the U.S., their primary market, they had a sales force that sold pri-marily to department store chains and specialty kitchen stores. U.S. dis-tribution was handled out of three distribution centers, located in South Carolina, Chicago, and Los Angeles. And that was the source of the CEO's concern: their distribution costs were very high, and he was considering closing the Chicago distribution center. He wanted a second opinion re-garding his decision.

We discussed their products and their sales process. We talked about their manufacturing plants, both in South Carolina and France. We re-viewed their distribution network and their fulfillment process. At some point in the conversation, he shared the financials from the previous year to highlight his concerns about distribution costs. A simplified version of the P&L is shown in Exhibit 1.

The CEO was right. Distribution costs seemed to be seriously out of line. 20% of revenue went to fund distribution. This likely should have been 5% to 8%. I asked more questions about the business and about the operations. We then went to lunch with his Vice President of Distribution. He echoed the CEO's concerns about the excessive cost of distribution, and he agreed with the idea of closing the Chicago distribution center.

After we returned from lunch, I asked the Distribution VP if he had some more detailed data on distribution costs, and he said that he would have it for me shortly. I then asked the CEO if I could meet for an hour with the Senior Vice President of Marketing, and then have an hour or so to look over the data by myself. I said that I would meet him back in his office at four o'clock, if that worked for him. "Fine by me," he replied.

Exhibit 1 - Le Creuset 1982 Profit & Loss Statement

Revenue		$25,000,000
Expense		
Cost of Goods Sold		
	Material	$2,500,000
	Labor	$8,500,000
Total		$11,000,000
Gross Margin		$14,000,000
%		56%
Distribution		$5,000,000
Facilities		$1,000,000
Sales & Marketing		$4,000,000
Management		$1,000,000
Total		$11,000,000
EBITDA		$3,000,000
%		12%

I met with the marketing SVP and then holed up in an empty conference room. At four o'clock, I returned to the CEO's office.

"I appreciate the candor which you and your people have shown today, and I was happy to find that a lot of relevant data was readily available. I think that has enabled me to come up with some interesting ideas," I said.

"First, I wouldn't be comfortable taking $350,000 of your money to conduct a thorough analysis of your distribution function," I began. "A quick analysis of your current sales volumes and distribution costs clearly shows that you should close both the L.A. and Chicago distribution centers and operate only one warehouse, here in Early Branch. South Carolina is clearly the optimal location because it abuts the manufacturing plant. There is no way that you can economically operate remote distribution centers with your current demand rates."

"Now," I continued, "I do have a good use for that $350,000. I think you should hire my partner, Gordon Ramseier, who is a very experienced and capable sales and marketing consultant. I was shocked by your unit demand history, both for cookware sets and for individual pieces," I continued. "You are a well-known company with, I suspect, very high brand awareness and a very strong reputation for quality. You have over 3,000 retail outlets for your product across the United States. And yet you only sold 25,000 sets and 30,000 individual pieces during all of 1984.

"Yes," I said, "you have a distribution cost problem. I estimate that, today, you could probably ship every retail order by Federal Express from your South Carolina warehouse, and still save money. But, in my judgment, your bigger opportunity is to grow demand through more effective sales and marketing. And Gordie can help you do that."

"That's very interesting," he responded. "Can you show me the numbers underpinning your conclusions in more detail?"

"Sure," I said, and I spent about an hour sharing my high-level analysis and my conclusions. Among other factors, I showed him Le Creuset's average sales per retail outlet. I compared that with my experience at past retail clients Target Stores and Service Merchandise. I reviewed my opinion on their current marketing strategy and their lack of an effective consumer advertising program. And I used their current P&L to project the financial implications of a 25% and a 50% increase in sales.

When I was done, he said, "I see what you mean. I respect your integrity for walking away from an easy $350,000, but I am eager to meet with Gordie. Will you help me set up the meeting?"

I did, and Gordie went on to complete several assignments for Le Creuset, all concerned with growing consumer demand. The company went on to double their U.S. sales over the next several years.

Rule #1: Define the underlying problem.

AVOID ALLOCATED COSTS

In 1978, my first assignment with Booz Allen was for NL Bearings, a subsidiary of NL Industries. They had two operating divisions; one headquartered in Toledo, Ohio, which manufactured sophisticated measuring devices that were very material-intensive; and one headquartered in Indianapolis, which manufactured precision machined parts that were very labor-intensive. Both supplied the oil drilling industry. We were retained to help them deal with the Indianapolis division, which they said was unprofitable.

Exhibit 2 shows a simplified profit and loss statement similar to the one we were given when we arrived and began work. As you can see, the Indianapolis operation was losing money while the Toledo division was profitable. The overall business, while profitable, was only marginally so. Management's plan was to close or sell Indianapolis and focus their attention on increasing the profitability of Toledo.

Exhibit 2: Profit & Loss Statement ($000)

	Toledo	Indianapolis	Total
Revenue	$285,000	$285,000	$570,000
Expenses			
Material	70,000	30,000	100,000
Labor	20,000	125,000	145,000
Engineering	85,000	85,000	170,000
Purchasing	35,000	35,000	70,000
Mgmt	30,000	25,000	55,000
Total	240,000	300,000	540,000
Profit	$45,000	($15,000)	$30,000
Margin	15.79%	-5.26%	5.26%

After a few days in the corporate offices, we spent two weeks visiting both operating divisions. We visited Toledo first and were generally unimpressed with the management team. There was a lot of work-in-process inventory in the factory. The workers didn't seem to be very productive. We had no facts at this point; just some first impressions.

Indianapolis, on the other hand, appeared to be a well-run operation. The organization seemed lean and appropriate. The factory workers seemed to be working efficiently. And the management team seemed to be experienced and knowledgeable; again, just a first impression.

When we got back to the corporate office, we began to tear apart the numbers. What had initially appeared to be direct costs for engineering, purchasing, and management were actually allocated corporate overhead costs, and they appeared to dominate the cost structure. We needed to understand and deconstruct them. Here is a simplified version of what we found:

Exhibit 3: Overhead Cost Breakdown ($000)

	Toledo	Indianapolis	Total
Overhead			
Division	$10,000	$5,000	$15,000
Corporate	140,000	140,000	280,000
Total	$150,000	$145,000	$295,000

As you can see, most of the overhead expenses were allocated corporate costs. We learned that overhead was allocated to the divisions based on their respective revenues. We then tore into the numbers. Exhibit 4 is another simplified version of what we found:

Exhibit 4: Corporate Overhead Breakdown ($000)

	Corporate	Toledo	Indy
Management	$20,000	$10,000	$10,000
Purchasing		60,000	10,000
Engineering		150,000	20,000
Total	$20,000	$220,000	$40,000

Corporate overhead was dominated by two functional departments: Engineering and Purchasing. And 75% to 80% of these resources were devoted to supporting the Toledo operation, which was not surprising given the nature of their products: sophisticated measuring devices. Conversely, Indianapolis manufactured high-precision, machined parts that required very little support from Engineering or Purchasing.

We restated the financials to properly apportion corporate overhead based on actual resources dedicated to each division, and to eliminate any charges that did not directly support it. We did not attempt to allocate any shared costs at the corporate level to either operating division. When we were done, a startling picture emerged.

Exhibit 5: Restated Profit & Loss Statement ($000)

	Toledo	Indianapolis	Total
Revenue	$285,000	$285,000	$570,000
Expenses			
Material	70,000	30,000	100,000
Labor	20,000	125,000	145,000
Division OH	10,000	5,000	15,000
Corp OH	220,000	40,000	260,000
Total	320,000	200,000	520,000
Contribution	($35,000)	$85,000	$50,000
Margin	-12.28%	29.82%	8.77%
Corporate Costs			$20,000
Net Profit			$30,000
Profit Margin			5.26%

Not only was the Indianapolis division profitable, it was very profitable. And when the Toledo operation had to account for all the resources they actually used, they were a big money loser. Conventional wisdom had it ass backwards. Rudy Sabatino, the CEO of NL Bearings, completely changed his view. He decided to close or sell the Toledo division and eliminate 75% of his corporate organization that only existed to support it. Had Rudy done the reverse, he would have created a much bigger problem than he already had.

While this example happened exactly as I described, I made up the numbers to make the analysis clear, simple, and easy to understand. As such, they are exaggerated to make the point. The real work was much more detailed and nuanced, but the conclusion was the same.

It has been my experience over years of consulting assignments that trying to allocate costs that are shared by products, customers, plants, or divisions—in order to calculate the product, customer, plant, or division profitability—is almost always an exercise in futility. And it often leads to erroneous conclusions and bad decisions. Better to deal with direct costs only and consider the results to be a contribution to shared costs and profit.

A GOOD AD CAN'T SELL A BAD PRODUCT

I was part of a team that did some interesting work for Cadillac in 1989. The team was led by my partner Len Sherman, and I was a Consulting Officer. Our assignment was to analyze the effectiveness of Cadillac's marketing function. Their sales had been declining and senior management thought that their problem was ineffective marketing. I was asked to get involved due to my extensive experience in the auto industry, although, if truth be told, most of my experience centered on operations and manufacturing. Len led the analysis and the thinking of the team. I merely kibitzed from the sidelines.

Len was puzzled by the analysis early in the project. By every measure, the various elements of Cadillac's marketing mix were solid: the advertising was effective, the reach was good, the message was on track, and the response was as expected. Print media was equally effective. So were public relations and marketing communications. Customer focus groups failed to signal any problems.

But the data suggested that something was wrong. Those pesky little facts showed that Cadillac's total U.S. new car sales had peaked in 1986, when 304,000 cars were sold. In 1989, when we were engaged on this assignment, their U.S. sales had dropped to 266,000—a 12.5% reduction.[9] Something was amiss. Len and the team decided to delve deeper into Cadillac's customer base to see if this would shed any light on the problem.

After looking at an array of data, the team discovered an interesting fact about Cadillac's recent customers. In 1986, their average customer was 55.1 years old. In 1987, the average customer was 56.4 years old. In one year, the average customer got 1.3 years older. Whoa! If that were an ongoing trend, that would be a very scary thing. The team then expanded the

---

[9] "Chrysler US Car Sales Figures," Carsalesbase.com, accessed October 2017, www.carsalesbase.com/us-car-sales-data/chrysler/.

analysis to see if something funny was going on. Exhibit 6 approximates what they found.

Over a ten-year period, the average age of the Cadillac customer had increased by twelve years. That meant their customer base was getting older and older, and would eventually die off. You could actuarially calculate the exact date that Cadillac would sell their last car to their last customer.

Exhibit 6: Average Age of a Cadillac Buyer

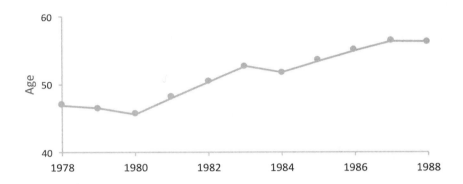

We did that. It was something like May 15, 2023.

That led the team to conclude that the problem with declining sales was caused by the product itself, not the marketing. We hypothesized that the problems were with design and quality. If you remember the late 1980s, Cadillac, and Lincoln for that matter, had those big, bulky cars that many younger people referred to as "tanks." And they had many issues with product quality ranging from fit and finish issues to engine and transmission problems. A series of focus groups confirmed our suspicions that design and quality were the true drivers of sales decreases.

We presented our findings to the management team at Cadillac, but they were slow to react. They didn't seem to grasp the urgency of their situation and the need for a timely and decisive departure from past practices.

Once again, defining the problem correctly, and using numbers to dimension it, was the key to understanding. Streamlining designs and improving quality were obvious solutions to the problem once it was accurately defined.

✳

Based on the experiences I had over my entire career, I could have easily offered fifty examples of correctly defining a problem. Many would have been counter-intuitive. Some would have been surprising. But all would have been fact-based and rooted in the analytics.

I chose these three for a reason. The Le Creuset case study dealt with the issue of tunnel vision. The client was so grounded in their past experience that they couldn't see the glaring issue of surprisingly low sales. Instead, they myopically focused on their cost structure and determined that their problem was with distribution. They needed to take a step back and look at the business itself before they started casting about for a problem.

In the NL Bearings example, I chose to address the issue of allocated costs. I've found this issue to be the underlying reason why so many clients initially misdiagnose their problems. Be very careful when you try to allocate shared costs. It will often lead you astray.

Finally, I used the Cadillac marketing case study to highlight Randy Wayne White's caution about "snatching at a conclusion in advance of data." This is, indeed, a dangerous shortcut. Nothing suggested that Cadillac had a problem in marketing except that their sales had declined. They neglected to really define their problem based on facts and data, and as a result, they leaped to the wrong conclusion.

Before a goad does anything else, he or she must define the problem: clearly, analytically, and unambiguously. Perhaps surprisingly, this is where most of their value will be added.

CHAPTER 5

CHALLENGE CONVENTIONAL THINKING

Imagination is more important than knowledge.
—ALBERT EINSTEIN

*It's the exquisite moment of anticipation that
separates discovery from revelation.*
—RANDY WAYNE WHITE

hange agents are above all else curious. They wonder why things are the way they are. They notice inconsistencies in logic and presentation. And they know that their initial hypotheses are often just plain wrong. As 19th century humorist Josh Billings once said: "The trouble with most folks isn't their ignorance. It's knowin' so many things that ain't so."

As a change agent, you've got to challenge your thinking at every turn: when you are trying to define the problem, when you are trying to graphically present the analysis, when you are contemplating solutions, and when you are trying to describe the solution. It's not just about the analytics; it's about the entire change process.

Effective change agents also tend to be very creative. They creatively and elegantly define problems and remedies. And they are just as creative in how they communicate the problem, the analysis, and the solution to others.

Finally, effective change agents need intellectual stimulation. Their minds are always engaged, and they need mental challenges. These can be achieved by using either an unstructured process such as brainstorming, or by a more structured process such as lateral thinking—using an indirect and creative approach, typically by viewing the problem in a new and unusual light.

These three factors—curiosity, creativity, and intellectual stimulation—combine to allow change agents to routinely challenge conventional thinking. The three case studies I present in this chapter show three different ways that conventional thinking was rejected.

SEPARATE THE NICKELS FROM THE DOLLARS

It is said that a penny saved is a penny earned. While this might be good advice, it is still, after all, just a penny. It is not a dollar. A change agent needs to ignore the pennies, the nickels, and the dimes, and go in search of the dollars. They need to find the real levers of performance: the areas of maximum impact. Many clients had trouble separating the nickels from the dollars.

"Our indirect labor costs are 5% higher than industry norms," they might say. "We have to do something."

Why? Is this variance important? Would getting costs in line with industry norms really change anything? Is this the first issue that needs to be addressed? Many clients thought the facts were speaking for themselves and went to work to change things without understanding what the facts were really saying.

When it comes to facts, context is of the utmost importance. We saw this in the Le Creuset case study. There was clearly an opportunity for the company to cut its distribution costs. But when placed in the context of the opportunity to grow sales and revenue, excessive distribution costs were not the first thing on which to focus.

In the 1980s, most hospitals had a very conservative table of authorities when it came to capital spending. For example, at Lakeland Regional Medical Center—a hospital where I did considerable consulting work—vice presidents could sign off on a $25,000 capital expenditure. The CEO's authority was capped at $50,000; any capital purchase greater than that amount required the approval of the board of directors.

Now, in and of itself, this wasn't necessarily a problem. I never saw a board turn down a reasonable capital request from a hospital CEO. But this policy did establish and reinforce a culture which held that capital costs should always be minimized. This probably goes back to the early days of the hospital industry when capital was raised primarily through philanthropy, and was therefore relatively scarce; while expenses were reimbursed on a cost-plus basis, defined as applying a standard profit mark-up to actual costs when determining the final price of a good or service. This was certainly not the situation in 1986.

That is one reason why you saw, and often still see, large central ancillary departments in a hospital, like Radiology and Pathology, which attempted to maximize the utilization of all capital assets and did not attempt to balance this objective with any other competing ones, such as reducing labor costs.

The practice seemed to be that there was no amount of complexity, no amount of patient inconvenience, and no amount of additional labor that could ever justify spending additional capital dollars. I know this was not truly the practice, but it sure felt that way sometimes.

Today's hospitals often use portable machines to take standard X-rays of inpatients. But thirty years ago, every X-ray was done in the central Radiology Department. Let's consider the process whereby, in 1986, a patient who was convalescing in the hospital received a chest X-ray:

Exhibit 7: X-Ray Process Flow Chart

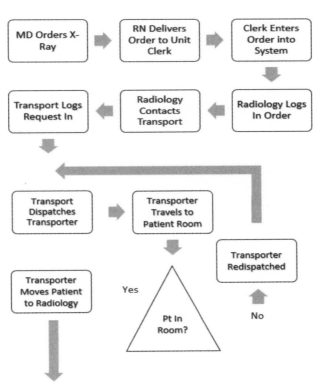

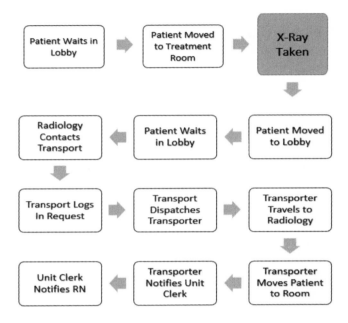

This process involved twenty-two different steps if the patient was in their room when the transport aide first arrived. If not, four steps were repeated multiple times until the patient could be found. Nine different hospital employees were required to perform this relatively simple task. Two different computer systems were used. And the patient had to wait upwards of forty-five minutes at various points during the process. And this did not even include the radiologist receiving the X-ray, reading it, and writing up and disseminating the diagnosis. Taking the actual X-ray was simply one step, and was usually the fastest to execute.

The apparent reason for this long and cumbersome process was to keep the radiology equipment fully utilized. The total compensation of the nine employees required to execute an X-ray order was about $400,000 per year, whereas the cost of a standard, basic X-ray machine was around $75,000. In the redesigned patient-focused hospital, we decentralized basic radiology by placing an X-ray machine on every nursing unit and cross-training the RNs and techs to take the X-rays. This eliminated sixteen of the twenty-one process steps, seven of the nine employees involved in the process, and all of the patient dislocation and wait time. Each X-ray machine paid for itself within six months.

The lesson of this chapter is to separate the nickels from the dollars.

Here is what that means in the context of this example: Hospital labor costs generally represented 55% of total hospital operating expenses. Capital costs—as captured by annual depreciation and amortization—were typically 5%. Minimizing capital costs by using ever more labor and creating complex, unwieldy processes was clearly not the answer.

The first thing you ought to do when you start to challenge the status quo is to separate the nickels from the dollars.

TRY THE OTHER END OF THE TELESCOPE

There were six offices at Burson-Marsteller that were an ongoing challenge for the firm's leadership team: Prague, Budapest, Kiev, Warsaw, Kuala Lumpur, and Bangkok. They all lost money, year-in and year-out. But Burson's business model required a complete global network to serve the communications needs of the firm's global clients. That meant we couldn't simply close them. Clients demanded a presence in each of these markets.

Each of these offices generated about $2 million in revenue and had about $2.25 million in operating costs, meaning that each one lost approximately $250,000 each year. As a firm, Burson had annual revenues of about $350 million and gross margins of about $35 million. So, these offices were not a major strategic issue. They were more of an embarrassment and a pain in the ass. The Corporate CFO was responsible for getting these offices profitable, and my predecessors and I devoted a disproportionate amount of time and energy trying to get this done.

There were several problems that were common across these offices. First, they were small. A $2 million office was subscale and a challenge to run efficiently. But the bigger problems had to do with the imposition of firm-wide service offerings and pricing policies that were not consistent with the realities of the markets in the countries where they operated. Thai, Hungarian, and Czech markets bore little resemblance to those of the U.S., France, or Japan. And yet corporate management pretended that they did.

As a simple example, public relations firms of old had provided a "clipping" service for their clients, whereby the firm would physically scan newspapers from around the country looking for any mention of the company or its products, and then would clip and send these materials to the client on a daily or weekly basis. In the 1980s and 1990s, the Internet and various new technologies made clipping services cost-ineffective and unnecessary in the U.S. But as late as 1998, they were still in demand in countries like Ukraine and the Czech Republic and could be sold if priced at national, not global, norms.

The firm tried all the normal responses to get these offices profitable: cost reduction programs, new management teams, new performance reports, and more frequent follow-up with the local Managing Director. Nothing worked. It looked like these losses were just going to be the cost of operating a global network.

Then I had a thought. If we simply gave the businesses away, we would avoid the operating losses. But we needed these offices to round out our global network. So, what if we made them franchises? We would give them to the Managing Directors and allow them to operate and price their businesses as they saw fit. But they would remain as part of the Burson family. And if we made their franchise fee a percentage of revenue, their contributions would always be positive. I decided to give it a try with one of the money-losing offices.

Burson-Marsteller's office in Prague had been in place for many years. It was led by a gentleman named Michal Donath, who was well-known and highly respected in business, government, and political circles in the Czech Republic. He was a trusted advisor to the Czech president and counted most large Czech companies among his clients. But the market for public relations and marketing communications had not yet evolved to that of other Western countries.

I phoned Michal and asked him to come to New York for a meeting. When he walked into my office a few days later, I imagine that he expected another ass-chewing about his poor financial performance.

Instead, I said, "Michal, have I got a deal for you! I propose to give you the Czech business lock, stock, and barrel. You can have the clients, the staff, the office, the furniture, the computers, everything. I will also give you all the cash that you now have in the bank. All of this will cost you nothing."

I continued: "We will make you an affiliate of the firm and give you a license to use our name. Your firm will be called Donath/Burson-Marsteller. We will give you the right of first refusal on any potential business in the Czech Republic. We will allow you to continue to use our e-mail system. You can send your employees to company training programs. You will still be part of the family. In most ways, it will feel like business as usual.

"But as the owner, you will have the freedom to sell any services you want for any price you deem appropriate. And you can compensate the staff however you see fit. The only requirements are that you provide quality service to all clients and that you will pay us a franchise fee of 15% of your total revenue each quarter. The rest is up to you.

"Finally," I said, "my best guess is that you will be the first person in the Burson-Marsteller family to make $1 million a year. That's five times what you are making now."

Michal was speechless. "Can you run that by me again?" he asked. So I did. You could almost hear the gears turning in his head.

Finally, Michal said, "I'm going to need to think about this. When do you need an answer?"

"Is next week okay?" I replied.

"You bet. And thanks."

I spoke with Michal several times over that next week, and we clarified a bunch of issues. The opportunities were clear, and over time, he got comfortable with the risks. A week later he called and said, "Let's do it!"

We got the lawyers involved and drew up an agreement. Several weeks later, we closed the deal and Michal was off to the races. Starting three months later, we began to receive quarterly checks from Michal. Initially, they were for maybe $75,000. Then they grew to over $100,000. The first year alone, we received about $400,000 in cash. And we no longer had to deal with a $250,000 loss. It was a $650,000 profit turnaround.

From Michal's standpoint, he could hire some less expensive staff and put them to work on lower-value, more commodity-like projects that were still in demand in the Czech Republic. He doubled the size of the business over a couple of years—partly because of the new service offerings and partly because he was the owner, and therefore more committed to the business's success. Shortly before the second anniversary of the deal, Michal happened to be in New York and stopped by my office. He thanked me profusely for giving him this opportunity, to which I said that we were pretty happy on our end too. He then said I had been right in my prediction. He was on pace to make over $1 million that year. I continue to get a Christmas card from Michal every year. His business continues to thrive.

I did similar deals with the managers of the other five money-losing offices. Two folded in the first year, and we had to find another franchisee. But the other three were successful.

Conventional wisdom and the normal approach to this problem of unprofitable operations is always to focus on the operations themselves, and perhaps change management or try productivity improvement programs or whatever. After months of beating my head against the wall, I decided to look at the situation in a new way. Sometimes it pays to turn the telescope around and look at things through the other end. Do not, however, try this with a horse.

DO NOT BE A BANKER

Accounts receivable is a very big deal in any professional partnership, be it a law firm, an accounting firm, a management consulting firm, or a roofing contractor. The working capital that is tied up in receivables is directly funded by the partners. Think about it. If a partnership has $1 million in outstanding receivables that have been on the books for sixty days, that represents $1 million in cash that could have been distributed to the partners sixty days ago had it been collected. Even worse, the probability of actually collecting the receivable goes down with each passing week.

Often, partners at professional service firms that are growing rapidly are surprised when their annual compensation doesn't increase—either proportionately or at all. The answer is frequently that the cash they otherwise would have received had to be used to fund the increase in accounts receivable.

Booz Allen Hamilton had billing policies that were like those of most other consulting firms. We would bill our clients for estimated professional fees and expenses thirty days in advance, and make clear that we expected payment within thirty days. That way, at the end of the month, the firm would receive a check at the same time it was paying employees and reimbursing them for out-of-pocket expenses. Theoretically, there would be no impact on cash flows.

Even though this was the policy, a few partners were sloppy about billing and collecting in a timely way. Total firm-wide receivables should have averaged thirty days if policies were adhered to and enforced. Actual receivables were more like fifty days. That meant each partner had several hundred thousand dollars of "their" cash tied up in working capital.

In 1982, I won a major supply chain management assignment at Service Merchandise Corporation in Nashville, Tennessee. They were one of the first catalog showroom retailers, offering fine jewelry, toys, sporting goods, and electronics.

Service Merchandise was well known for its unusual shopping experience, which emphasized the catalog, even within the stores. Customers would enter the showroom and receive a tablet which included an order form to record the catalog numbers of desired items. Most items were displayed in the showroom, allowing customers to see and handle products as they shopped. But Service Merchandise catalogs were also placed in strategic locations throughout the store to allow customers to shop for items that were not on display. When ready to place their orders, customers would take the tablet to a cashier, who would collect the payment and submit the order to the store's stockroom. The customer would then move to the merchandise pickup area near the exit, where the order would emerge from the stockroom on a conveyor belt.

This assignment was very competitive. Service Merchandise had requested proposals from fourteen different firms. The field was narrowed to two and both were asked to make presentations to the Chairman & CEO, Raymond Zimmerman, and his senior staff. The first presentation was made by Deloitte & Touche, who had the strongest retail consulting practice in the country. This assignment was going to be led by their national practice leader, Randy Allen, a recognized industry expert.

Booz Allen was the other firm selected to present. I didn't have any experience in the retail industry, and I was just beginning to build a national reputation in service operations. But I did have considerable functional expertise in supply chain management. At the end of my presentation, I turned and spoke directly to the CEO.

"Raymond," I said. "Let me make this very easy for you. If you want the very best industry solution for your company, hire Deloitte & Touche. Randy Allen is the best there is. But if you want the best functional solution, hire us. We truly understand supply chain management as a functional discipline."

"Give me an example," Raymond asked.

"I will," I responded. "I assume you are familiar with open-to-buy systems. If Randy gets the work, you will end up with the best, most advanced open-to-buy system in the industry. But if we do the work, I will convince you that open-to-buy systems are conceptually flawed and you should have no part of them." (An open-to-buy system, which was then common in the retail industry, constrained buyers from purchasing more merchandise than was sold over a rolling three-month period. This was an illogical process that stopped buyers from reordering hot-selling merchandise to compensate for slow-moving inventory that they had over-bought in the past. Here is an example: Let's suppose our buyer has an open-to-buy limit of $1 million. She buys $500,000 of red shoes, $400,000 of blue shoes, and $100,000 of green shoes. The red and blue shoes are duds and don't sell. But the green shoes are a big hit and sell out within two days. Because she has $900,000 tied up in blue and red shoe inventory, her open-to-buy is only $100,000. Even though the green shoes sold at a rate of $50,000 per day, she is precluded from ordering more than a two-day supply. Said another way, two dumbs don't make a smart.)

We were excused from the room and awaited a decision. Raymond left the conference room and asked me to come with him. We went to his office where he said: "You got the assignment. Don't disappoint me."

"I won't," I replied, "and thank you very much."

"There is just one thing in your proposal that has to be changed," Raymond continued. "I will not pay estimated fees and expenses in advance. Never have! Never will!"

"Well, Raymond, that's going to be a problem," I said.

"Take it or leave it!" he replied.

"Before we go there, let me tell you my issue. You are a world-class retailer. But I'd bet money that you'd be a pretty crummy banker. I am an outstanding management consultant, but I know that I'd be a horrible banker too. By billing you thirty days in advance, and asking you to pay at the end of the month, I don't put either one of us in the position of being a banker to the other. We get paid at the same time as we're paying our people. Otherwise, either I am funding you or you are funding me."

Raymond sat quietly and thought for a few minutes. Then he said: "I understand what you just said. It makes good sense. But I still will not pay estimated fees in advance."

"Well," I said, "how about if I bill you at the end of the month for actual fees and you process the payment within a week?" I could live with five-day receivables.

"I've got a better idea," Raymond offered. "On the last day of every month, you plan to be in Nashville. At nine o'clock in the morning, you come to my office and give me your monthly invoice. I will approve it and have a check for you by lunch. That way, neither of us is a banker to the other. Do I have it right?"

"You sure do!" I said. And for the next eighteen months, that's exactly what we did. Zero receivables, just like it was supposed to be.

Another problem solved with a little imagination.

✳

It's hard to coach people to challenge their thinking about a problem, a solution, or a communications strategy. The first case study suggested trying to keep facts in perspective. Yes, capital costs in a hospital are a big deal. It's just that labor costs are a ten-times bigger deal. Use facts to challenge your thinking about the apparent problem and the tempting solution.

In the second case study, I chose a problem whose solution defied conventional wisdom. Who would have ever thought you could simply give a business away, and with it the problems and operating losses? I really had to challenge my thinking, and operate beyond my base of experience, to envision this solution.

Finally, I shared the imaginative solution that the CEO of Service Merchandise Corporation, Raymond Zimmerman, and I came up with to ensure that neither of us was acting as a banker to the other.

It was Roger von Oech who said that "creative thinking involves imagining familiar things in a new light, digging below the surface to find previously undetected patterns, and finding connections among unrelated phenomena." Try to suspend your belief about how things are, and instead ponder how they could be. Keep your thinking simple and uncluttered. Remember Occam's razor: The simplest explanation is usually the right one. This is the essence of the challenge.

CHAPTER 6

LIVE YOUR VALUES

Never be bullied into silence. Never allow yourself to be made a victim.
Accept no one's definition of your life; define yourself.
—HARVEY FIERSTEIN

When I was about seventeen years old, my father sat me down and said the following: "Son, you are reaching an age where you have to decide how much your integrity is worth. You are going to be given many opportunities to sell your integrity, and you really need to decide in advance just how much it is worth. For example, suppose you buy something that costs $6.50 and you give the cashier a ten-dollar bill. Then suppose she gives you change for a twenty—an extra ten dollars. Do you keep the money or give it back to the cashier and say, "I think you gave me too much back?" If you keep it, you just sold your integrity for a measly ten bucks. I don't know about you, but my integrity is worth a lot more than that."

He continued: "Now, if I could find a way to cheat on my taxes for $1 million, and thought that I could get away with it, I might do it. I think that $1 million is a pretty fair price for my integrity. But ten dollars, or a hundred dollars, or a thousand dollars, I'll keep my integrity, thank you very much. You need to figure out your price in advance before temptation clouds your judgment." This was some of the best advice I ever received.

Clearly, I would not then, nor would I now, sell my integrity for any price. If I did, it would serve to change my fundamental character. It would compromise my core values. That said, my father's challenge was very useful to me in putting the abstract notion of integrity into a real-world context. It made me think about, and helped me to define, my value system.

I find that integrity in business, while not rare, is too often compromised:

a little cheat here; a little lie there. Tell the boss what she wants to hear, even though you know it to be untrue. Consciously avoid data that doesn't support your conclusion. Tell someone they are a valued member of the team and then terminate them a few weeks later when it is convenient for you.

As a change agent, you cannot afford to have your integrity compromised. It is the basis on which all else is built.

ETHICS MATTER

Over my career, I encountered a few business associates that I thought were unethical. Not that they committed fraud or broke the law. They just behaved in a way that I considered unethical, defined in the dictionary as "not in accord with the standards of a profession, or unwilling to adhere to proper rules of conduct."[10]

The first one that comes to mind is a former client from Los Angeles. He was, and is, very well-known in business, social, and philanthropic circles. To preserve his anonymity and avoid lawsuits, let's call him Ed Brody. Ed was the CEO of a big Fortune 500 company, and he had given millions to very good causes. That said, I'm a bit skeptical. I know first-hand that he is an egotist of the highest order. And he is into power and control. Lots of business executives fit this mold, but Ed was the poster child.

In 1991, his company was having some serious performance problems in their operations. Let's call them Viper Industries. At the time, I was the Service Operations Practice Leader at Booz Allen, and so I was the natural one to respond when Ed asked us for help.

I flew to Los Angeles and met with Mr. Brody for several hours. His personality was a little grating, and he struck me as a bit of a self-centered jerk: he liked to talk about himself and brag about his accomplishments. But I had worked with similar folks before, and it was no big deal. I returned to New York and wrote a proposal for how Booz Allen would help him address his problems, and then flew to Los Angeles again to present our proposal to him.

On this trip, he warmed up considerably and was enthusiastic when he said that, after reviewing several other proposals, he was awarding the work to us. We were, he said, more experienced and more qualified than the other major firms to whom he had spoken. I was growing fonder of Ed by the minute.

---

[10] "unethical," Dictionary.com, 2017, accessed June 2017, www.dictionary.com.

The assignment was a major one for the firm. As I recall, I had priced the first phase at $750,000. I assigned four client service staff members to the work and estimated that it would take three months to complete. I also thought that our involvement would likely be required for a year or so after that to assist in implementing the suggested restructuring, and I told that to Mr. Brody up front.

We had been working on the assignment for two weeks when I took the staff out for a well-deserved team dinner. They had been busting their butts, and things were going very well with the client. After dinner, I retired to the hotel bar for a nightcap and some alone time. I wound up sitting next to a guy about my age—let's call him Brad—and we struck up a conversation.

At some point, I asked him what he did.

"I'm a management consultant," he answered.

"You're kidding," I replied. "I am too."

"Yeah, I'm a partner with McKinsey out of Chicago."

"I'll be damned. I'm a partner with Booz Allen in New York."

"Are you out here on client work?" he asked.

"Yes, I'm leading an assignment for a company just a couple of blocks away."

"What a coincidence," Brad said. "So am I."

This was beginning to get eerie. "Is it north or south of here?" I asked. "North."

"I shouldn't ask this, but is it Viper Industries?"

"Yes, it is," he said.

We went on talking. After about fifteen minutes, it became obvious that good old Ed had hired McKinsey & Company to do the same exact work as we had been retained to do. All his comments about our experience and qualifications distinguishing us from our competitors were a bunch of bull. Mr. Brody wanted to have a bake-off, meaning that two of us would do the same assignment and the one who did it the best would get the $2–$3 million of follow-on work.

Now I don't have anything against a bake-off. I love competition as much as the next guy. And not to toot my own horn, but over my twenty-five-year consulting career, I never lost a competitive assignment to McKinsey & Company. I would have been happy to have participated in a bake-off, if only Ed had told me—and Brad—up front.

The essence of any professional services relationship is mutual trust.

It applies to all such providers: doctors, lawyers, consultants, accountants. The client must trust the provider to offer honest, informed counsel. And the provider must trust the client to tell the truth—all the time. This is the only way such a professional relationship can work.

I told Brad, "I have good news for you. At eight o'clock tomorrow morning, I am resigning from this assignment. I can't work for a client who plays games behind my back. To hell with him—it's all yours. Good luck with Eddie."

Brad said that were it up to him, he would resign too. Unfortunately, he was a junior partner and could not make this decision on his own. He said he was going back to his room to make some calls. I have no idea what McKinsey decided to do, but I hope they also told old Ed Brody to stick it.

At precisely eight o'clock the next morning, I showed up at Ed's office. "I'm sorry, Kurt, but I have meetings scheduled nonstop all morning. Can we speak this afternoon?" he asked.

"This will only take a minute."

"Okay."

"Ed, last night I think I learned that you hired McKinsey & Company to do the same exact assignment that you hired us to do—sort of a bake-off for the next phase of work. Is that true?" I asked.

"Well, Kurt, so what if I did? It's my company."

"Ed, I've got late-breaking news: McKinsey wins the bake-off, because we resign. Your behavior is one of the sleaziest things a client has ever done to me. And even worse, you were willing to piss a million dollars of your stockholders' money down the drain just to play your little game. I'll send you an invoice for our time and expenses to date. And I strongly, make that *very strongly*, suggest that you pay it promptly."

I went down to our team room and announced that we were through at Viper and that everyone should go back to the hotel, pack up, and catch the next flight home. And since it was Thursday, I told them to take Friday off and have some fun.

By the time I got back to the New York office, the story was already out. Apparently, Ed had called a couple of senior partners he knew and demanded my head. One in particular, Joe Nemec, was furious and claimed that I had called a valued client a sleaze ball.

"He is a sleaze ball, Joe," I said. "But I didn't call him that. I accused him of sleazy behavior, and of that, he is 100 percent guilty. He is unethical, pure and simple. And by the way, if you are going to demand that I be fired, ask our colleagues which of us they would rather have as a partner, me or Ed Brody? I'll take my chances."

I never heard another word about it, although it was added to the lore of the firm. And good old Ed paid my invoice in full.

YOU'RE KNOWN BY THE COMPANY YOU KEEP

I was elected to the Booz Allen partnership in 1984, six years after joining the firm. I was honored and humbled. Maybe one out of twenty folks hired by the firm ever becomes a partner. This was the highlight of my professional career.

There were many benefits to being a partner in a firm like Booz Allen. You had the chance to work with blue-chip clients and take on interesting challenges on their behalf. You had the opportunity to work with some very smart and experienced people. You learned new things every day. You could hire and develop dynamite young people who kept you on your toes. The money was great too.

But perhaps most important, you were part of a community of professionals who shared a common work ethic, a commitment to client service, and a strong value system. This is what made the partnership cohesive and enduring.

The value system consisted of mutual trust, respect, honesty, and integrity among the partner corps. Partners told each other the truth, even when it was difficult or uncomfortable. They respected other partners' views, even when they disagreed with them. Partners knew that their colleagues had their back. It was a very healthy culture.

Unfortunately, in the late 1980s, the leadership of the firm began to compromise their value system for short-term gains, mostly driven by pressure to increase partner compensation. An eroding and compromised value system usually takes many years to destroy an organization. So it was with Booz Allen. In 2008, some twenty years after the initial compromises began, the firm was divided. The technology business was sold to the Carlyle Group and the commercial business remained independent and was renamed Booz & Company.

Six years later, Booz & Company was sold to PricewaterhouseCoopers, and it has since been integrated and subsumed into the whole. It no longer exists as a stand-alone entity.

While many contend that the demise of the firm was driven by the greed of the then-senior partners, I believe that one major reason for the firm's failure was a series of value system abuses that began in the late 1980s. The erosion of trust, respect, and collegiality caused key partners to leave the firm, which ultimately resulted in poor and unsustainable financial performance.

I was elected to the firm's board of directors in 1989, and I served on it for three years. At that time, the board was usually comprised of eight senior partners who ran various parts of the firm—the CEO, the Managing Partner of the U.S. commercial business, the Managing Partner of the technology business, and the leaders of Europe and Asia, for example. There were also seven client service partners who rounded out the board of fifteen directors.

The board was the governing body of the firm. It set the strategy of the firm, it set policy, it selected the CEO, it approved new partner elections, and it got involved in major decisions proposed by the management team.

Every year the commercial business partners around the world would recruit at top business schools and would hire many newly minted MBAs to be based out of various offices and regions. There was always a forecast made of how many graduates with an offer would accept it and how many would turn it down. Thus, for example, if I wanted to bring ten new associates into the Service Operations practice, I might make fifteen offers and plan for a 66% acceptance rate.

At one board meeting, Martin Waldenstrom, the Managing Partner of the worldwide commercial business, reported that the acceptance rate on MBA job offers was running unusually high that year, and that we were already significantly over-subscribed. But, he went on to say, Stanford University had a later recruiting cycle than other schools, and while we had made twelve job offers there, no one had yet accepted or declined. Thus, he suggested, we should simply pull the offers from the Stanford students so as not to worsen the problem.

Discussion ensued.

Several partners probed the economics of the situation and the alternatives. There was general agreement that this problem was already likely to cause partner bonuses to remain flat or even decline slightly for the year. If we took on eight or ten Stanford MBAs, the situation would be that much worse.

Others talked about our reputation at the top-ranked business schools—not just Stanford, but Harvard and Northwestern and Carnegie Mellon—once word got out about what we had done.

Both sides debated the issue for some time. Finally, I couldn't hold back. "Colleagues," I said, "this is not about our bonuses or our reputation. It is about our value system. We made the forecasting mistake, and now we want to make twelve young Stanford students pay for it. What about our integrity? What about our self-respect? For me, this is a non-starter. We should just absorb the extra staff and move on."

Martin turned to me and said: "You don't get it, Kurt. We have a business to run here."

The board voted thirteen to two to withdraw the job offers from the Stanford students. I was ashamed.

My first year on the board, we decided to radically change the compensation system for the partners. In the past, there was no disciplined system for determining partner salaries. Raises were based on current salaries as much as merit and equity. And bonuses, while linked to performance, were subjective and did not reflect a true partnership. Partners tended to compete with one another and often tried to differentiate their performance from that of their peers—bookings (sales), billability, staff development.

All that changed in 1989. We adopted a "slot-based" compensation system, whereby each partner would be put into one of twelve compensation slots. A new partner would begin in slot 1. Thereafter, he would be periodically reviewed and would be moved through the slots based on his tenure and performance. Each slot had a predetermined number of compensation points—one hundred for a slot 1 to three hundred for a slot 12. Each year, distributable income would be divided pro rata among the partners based on the total compensation points of all the partners. This meant that the highest paid partner would receive three times the annual compensation of a newly-minted partner. And it also meant that the only way for a partner to affect their compensation in a given year was to grow the overall firm and make it more profitable. Internal competition was out; cooperation was in.

The new compensation system was going to be a major challenge for the older, longer-term partners. Performance metrics for partners had changed, and personal contributions to team successes were now the primary driver of their compensation. Some of them would be taking home less money than they had in the past. And some would be unable to adapt to the new environment.

When this matter came before the board, our chairman, Mike McCulloch, proposed that we put a three-year moratorium on terminating partners for lack of performance. He wanted to calm the fears of many senior partners and allow them time to grow into the new way of doing things.

Several of us were against this approach. "This is not a social club," I argued. "Partners should succeed or fail based on their performance. Period! There are no do-overs in a business like this. They need to step up. This is the big leagues."

As I recall, the vote was eleven to four in favor of the moratorium.

Just one year later, the board was asked to approve the forced termination of six partners whose performance had been sub-par for several years. This proposal just happened to coincide with a forecast of annual distributable income that showed total partner compensation declining slightly from the year before.

"This is outrageous," I said when the board was asked for comments. "I argued against the moratorium a year ago, and I was soundly voted down. Now, greed is causing you to change your mind. We gave our word and we can't take this action."

The debate continued and one board member suggested that these six partners would not be surprised and probably saw the handwriting on the wall some time ago.

"I'm not worried about these six partners," I countered. "I'm worried about everyone who is left; particularly the staff. We show ourselves to be completely lacking in honesty and integrity. We don't keep our word. Is this the example we want to set?" I was pissed.

Once again, the board voted ten to five to approve management's decision. Once again, I was ashamed. But this time I decided to act. A few months later, I resigned. My partners asked if I had a better offer. "No," I said. "I don't know what I am going to do. I just know that I don't want to do it here."

✳

If a change agent fails to stay true to a principled value system or if they compromise their integrity, they will quickly be found out. Change agents are always out in front leading the parade, and as such, they are very visible and closely watched. Anyone who is resisting the change agent's agenda is eagerly waiting for a way to challenge their credibility or their character.

In the first case study, Ed Brody didn't really do anything illegal. But he revealed his lack of honesty and integrity, and in my view, behaved unethically. I have never needed money enough to make me work with clients that I don't trust.

The second two case studies were more problematic. In the late 1980s and 1990s, Booz Allen Hamilton was not growing revenue and margins in a fashion that met the partners' annual income expectations. And a weak management team succumbed to peer pressure and compromised their values for short-term gains. Unfortunately, in my view, this ultimately led to the demise of the firm. Too many talented partners opted to leave the firm.

It was Michelle Obama who said during the 2016 presidential election: "When they go low, we go high." Successful goads always value their integrity and don't sell it for less than it is worth. And they don't compromise their values, particularly not for short-term gains. Remember: value system compromises always have consequences.

In this first section, *The Change Agent's Handbook*, I've tried to articulate six keys to successful change agency:
1. Build Disciples
2. Lead from the Front
3. Get Their Attention
4. Define the Problem
5. Challenge Conventional Thinking
6. Live Your Values

Surprisingly, most of these actions are rooted in relationships and behaviors: building and gelling a team, communicating with colleagues and clients, leading and adapting, and staying true to a solid value system.

It's also worth noting that I've said nothing about developing solutions. In my experience, if the problem is correctly and analytically defined, the solution is usually self-evident. In my prime, people would often ask me: "So don't management consultants help their clients find solutions to their problems?" I would generally respond: "No. We help them define their problems."

In the next section, I will discuss building a tool kit, wherein I will suggest the greatest areas of leverage for creating transformative change to improve business performance.

THE CHANGE AGENT'S TOOL KIT

My name is Sherlock Holmes. It is my business
to know what other people don't know.
—ARTHUR CONAN DOYLE

There are always many areas of any business that could benefit from change. But given that resources are always scarce, particularly among those able to envision and lead transformational change, companies are often reluctant to allocate adequate resources to such change initiatives, and change agents must prioritize their efforts. There are only six or seven basic areas offering sustainable improvement opportunities in the performance of most businesses. These are where the leverage almost always exists. And this is where the change agent's focus should be.

Before we begin to explore these points of leverage, we need to cover some basics that I've found helpful in thinking about the change process.

First, outcomes cannot be managed. They are what results after the managing is done. For example, you can't simply reduce cost. You usually need to focus instead on managing processes and resource utilization. To increase revenue, you might focus on marketing, sales, or price. To improve quality, you almost always start with processes, compliance, or product design. And finally, to improve profit, you need to reduce cost or increase revenue, which, in turn, means managing utilization, processes, marketing, price, compliance, and product design. Too many folks try to manage outcomes instead of directing their effort to the factors that drive those outcomes.

Second, it is important to scope the initiative. A change agent may limit his or her attention to incremental change: reengineering processes, increasing utilization, or increasing price, for example. Or they may focus on transformational change: changing the basis of competition, monetizing value creation, decompartmentalizing processes, or reducing product and operational complexity.

When carefully designed, developed, and implemented, each of these initiatives can provide sustainable results. But too often, companies and change agents focus on the program du jour, like productivity improvement or cost reduction. Such efforts rarely provide sustainable benefits. As Larry Taylor says, "A program is a short-term solution to a long-term problem."[11]

I present case study examples of both incremental and transformational change initiatives in this section. In the next section, I review a seminal transformational change initiative.

---

[11] Taylor, *Be an Orange,* 54.

CHAPTER 7

CHALLENGE THE VALUE PROPOSITION

*We must maintain a value proposition to our customers as well as
differentiate the Starbucks Experience. That is the key.*
—HOWARD SCHULTZ

Usually, the most highly-leveraged opportunity for sustained improvement in any company, and the one least often pursued, is to challenge and alter the basic value proposition of the business. Many companies do not even articulate their value proposition. They behave as if it is self-evident.

A value proposition asserts a company's reason for being. What products or services will they provide? To what customers will they provide them? And how will they create tangible value for these customers? A value proposition is strategic. It needs to be specific and precise. It must be competitively differentiated. And as such, it must be externally focused.

Often, circumstances change and a company's value proposition becomes outdated. Think about Barnes & Noble post-Amazon. Their old, bricks-and-mortar value proposition would not allow them to effectively compete with Amazon. It had to evolve. A company's value proposition needs to be regularly challenged and, at times, dramatically changed.

DO WE ADD ANY VALUE?

In 1992, shortly after we formed The Mead Point Group, Tom Curren, Senior Vice President of Planning for Marriott Corporation, called me to say that one of their operating units needed some outside help. I had built a relationship with Tom that went back six or seven years. This was the second time that it paid off.

My partner Stephen Baum and I met with Tony Alibrio, President of the Marriott's Health Care Division, at his office in Avon, Connecticut. His business provided contract food service management to hospitals throughout North America, generating at that time perhaps $2 billion in annual revenue and a 30% gross margin.

I remember that I was blown away when Tony said: "I need to know if we provide any real value to our clients." When a hospital contracted with them, Marriott would provide the management team and support staff who would then run the day-to-day food service operation for the hospital. Marriott would provide onsite managers and nutritionists. The hospital would continue to provide the kitchen, would pay for the groceries using Marriott's heavily discounted national prices, and would employ the hourly labor. Marriott simply managed the operation. And for that, they charged a healthy monthly fee.

Tony wanted to know if the value they provided to their hospital clients was greater than the fees they charged them. If they aren't, he said, "I had damn well better be the first one on the planet to know it." That was one of the most bold, enlightened, forward-looking, strategic questions I was ever asked by a client. He thought that they provided value, but he couldn't prove it.

We wrote a proposal which described how we would go about validating Marriott's value proposition. Tony approved it and we set to work. We had two Marriott employees assigned to us full-time for the duration of the project, which lasted about three months. We began by selecting ten of their client hospitals and ten hospitals that managed their own food service operations to form a basis for comparison of the value created by the management teams in both groups.

Because of my past work on the Patient-Focused Hospital initiative (discussed in the next section), I knew the CEOs of many successful hospitals around the country. Most were willing to participate in this cross-institutional analysis if they were given access to the results at the end. They were curious to see how they stacked up against their peers. And of course, we agreed to that condition.

Without going into laborious detail about the various analyses we performed, they were based on each individual hospital's historical food costs, labor costs, labor hours, labor utilization, menu offerings, nutritional programs, patient satisfaction surveys, and other pertinent indicators of performance and efficiency. Then we normalized the data so that we could compare performance across hospitals of differing sizes and volumes. Finally, we adjusted the data to account for the difference in nominal wage rates and other factor costs across the various geographies of the sample hospitals. (E.g., a food service worker in New York City would make more per hour than one in Lakeland, Florida.) We also conducted individual interviews with managers, nutritionists, and workers at all the twenty hospitals under review.

The results of this analysis were clear. The answer to Tony's original question—do we provide measurable value to our clients—was sometimes yes, sometimes no. In 70% of the Marriott-managed hospitals we studied, their cost and quality performance exceeded that of the self-managed hospitals. But in 30% of the Marriott-managed hospitals, performance fell well below that which these hospitals could have likely achieved on their own.

Based on our qualitative interviews, we posited the cause of the performance shortfalls: the quality of the onsite team, particularly the manager. When the manager was strong, the performance was usually solid, and real value was created for the client. When the manager was weak, performance was subpar and no value was created. I guess this isn't surprising given the nature of the contract management services business. But it was very eye-opening for Tony and his team.

It caused them to rethink many their internal processes and procedures. They completely revamped their hiring process by making it much more rigorous and pulling more line managers into it. They put a renewed emphasis on training programs for frontline managers and supervisors. They began to routinely capture performance metrics from each client operation similar to the ones used in our analysis, and created a system for benchmarking individual hospital performance against company targets. Finally, they began a more rigorous program of proactively identifying and removing local managers with substandard performance.

This is another example of the futility of trying to manage outcomes. We provided Tony with the insight that the local management of any given operation was the only substantive factor in causing outcomes to be what they were. It was these local managers who determined whether Marriott's value proposition would be fulfilled or not.

Here is an interesting anecdote about this work for Marriott. When we presented our proposal to Tony Alibrio, he commented that, based on our professional fees, he could see that both Stephen and I had about the same annual income as he did. That was not a problem, he said, but what bothered him was that we got paid in full regardless of the value received by Marriott, whereas a lot of his compensation came in the form of an annual bonus, awarded only if he met certain objectives and performance metrics. I told him that we would discuss his issue and get back to him.

Stephen and I talked it over on the way back to Greenwich. When I got to my office, I called Tony and asked him about Marriott's bonus process. He told me that the target bonus for a Division President was 20% of their base salary, but that they could earn up to 40% if they exceeded their annual performance targets. I then proposed the following deal to Tony. He could put 20% of our fees into an escrow account and hold them until he received his annual bonus. If he received his target bonus, we would receive the amount in escrow. If he fell short, our 20% would be proportionately reduced. But if he received a larger bonus, our 20% would be proportionately increased.

He responded by saying that this approach would not be fair to us, since we had no ability to influence most aspects of his job and his performance. I told him that if we were going to be partners, then each of us had to trust the other to do their jobs, and that we were happy to trust him if he would trust us. "Okay, if you're happy, I'm happy," he replied.

Three months after we finished the work, Tony called and asked us to meet him for dinner in Avon. He said that he had some issues that he wanted to talk about. We met the following week and talked about several issues over dinner. As we were drinking our after-dinner coffee, Tony said that he had recently received his annual bonus and was happy to report that he had been awarded the maximum of 40% of his base salary. Then he reached into his suit jacket pocket and pulled out a check. "This is for you guys," he said. It was a check for double the 20% of our fees that had been held in escrow. Tony was beaming from ear to ear as he gave us our "bonus." We shook hands and ordered a celebratory drink. As I recall, our fees for the project were $400,000. That means that Tony held back 20% or $80,000. And when all was said and done, we had doubled our eighty thousand. Good deal!

CHANGE THE GAME

In 2002, two years after I had retired, I got a call from a good friend and fellow management consultant. Ron Dreskin had been a senior executive for a major New York academic medical center. In the mid-1990s, he decided to leave his job and form his own consulting firm—Integrated Healthcare Solutions—focused on hospitals and physician groups.

Ron had received a call from Dr. Eric Rose, a world-class heart surgeon who was also the Chief of the Department of Surgery at Columbia-Presbyterian Hospital in Manhattan. He wanted to speak with Ron about a major strategic issue: how can the cardiac surgery group at Columbia-Presbyterian monetize their intellectual capital? Ron decided he could use some help with this one and asked me if we could work together on this. "I'm your guy!" I said.

We met with Eric several times to discuss the project. His issue was simply that he didn't see how he could sustain the excellence of Columbia-Presbyterian's cardiac surgery group, and of Columbia Medical School's cardiac surgery faculty, if his only revenue came from surgical procedures compensated at rates approved by insurance companies or Medicare. The compensation of his surgeons and his hospital would ultimately be no greater than that of a smaller community hospital in the same area, even though his surgeons were regularly making clinical breakthroughs and his hospital was offering leading-edge care. "I don't see how we can make it if we keep getting paid by the pound," he said, "particularly since our costs are of necessity higher than those of smaller community hospitals." Hospitals like Columbia-Presbyterian incur higher costs by virtue of their research, their teaching mission, and the generally higher acuity of their patients.

Eric approved our proposal for the first phase of work, and put together a working group consisting of him and two other surgeons to participate in and oversee our work. Dr. Craig Smith was, and still is, a world-renowned heart surgeon. He was nominally in charge of the cardiac surgery unit at Columbia-Presbyterian. Dr. Mehmet Oz was also a world-renowned heart surgeon. You know him today for his highly-rated TV show, *Dr. Oz*. Eric, Craig, and Mehmet came together to work with us on this challenging and stimulating project: How can Columbia-Presbyterian Hospital and the Columbia Medical School monetize the considerable intellectual capital and know-how imbedded in their cardiac surgery group, and thereby change their fundamental operating economics? Heady stuff!

We set to work analyzing everything about the cardiac surgery unit: their volumes, their revenue, their costs, and their outcomes. Then we tried to put all of this into a competitive context. There is a ton of data surrounding the hospital industry, mostly because of Medicare reporting. We could see just how they stacked up against their competition.

Columbia-Presbyterian had volumes, revenues, and costs that were proportionately consistent with those of other major hospitals in the New York area. This, we expected. But we also expected to see that their outcomes were superior, given the reputations of their key surgeons. We didn't see this. Their outcomes, while very good, were not demonstrably better than those of other large hospitals, either in New York or across the country. As a group, however, the large hospitals did generate better outcomes than smaller hospitals.

We then looked at their so-called intellectual capital and tried to articulate specific know-how and techniques that Columbia-Presbyterian surgeons had developed and pioneered. Given the information-sharing that is commonplace in the healthcare industry, it was difficult to isolate their unique contributions. But we were able to pull an impressive array of advances together.

Finally, we commissioned some market research into the national cardiac surgery market and Columbia-Presbyterian's reputation in it. By all measures, they enjoyed a superior reputation and were considered to be among the top four or five cardiac programs in the country, likely because of their strong brand and their contribution to advances in the field.

Ron and I presented all of our findings to Eric, Craig, and Mehmet; and the five of us set about brainstorming options. We quickly eliminated attempting to persuade Medicare or the insurance companies to compensate Columbia procedures at a higher rate. That seemed to be an obvious non-starter. We also rejected approaches to trying to patent know-how and charging for its use. This was not only hard to envision, but also would be inappropriate in the medical field.

After several meetings and several false starts, we hit upon a promising idea. We could sell the Columbia-Presbyterian cardiac care "system" and the Columbia Medical School brand to other hospitals around the country. Here are the elements of the value proposition that we finally defined. A client hospital would receive five deliverables:

1. An annual audit of their cardiac surgery program conducted on-site by an experienced Columbia-Presbyterian surgeon.
2. Quarterly meetings in New York to review new developments and know-how created by Columbia surgeons and staff.

3. The opportunity to assign one surgeon each year for a six-month rotation in the Columbia-Presbyterian cardiac ORs, working under the guidance and supervision of a senior Columbia surgeon.
4. Written protocols of most cardiac procedures and of appropriate post-operative care.
5. The ability to brand themselves as "A Columbia Heart Hospital."

We thought that they could price such an offering at $1 million, at least, and perhaps $2 million per hospital per year.

That concluded our Phase I work. We proposed a Phase II effort to further refine the proposed value proposition; discuss it with several hospital CEOs; work with Eric, Mehmet, and Craig to identify and try to sell it to several actual hospital clients; and finally, to put together a plan for how to turn this into a sustainable business. The group approved this additional work.

After the refinement was complete, we decided to take the show on the road. Eric and Ron were instrumental in getting audiences with high-potential hospital CEOs. These would be hospitals that were known for quality and service, but were number two or number three in their market in terms of size and utilization. The CEOs needed to be progressive and open to innovative ideas.

Collectively, over four months, Eric, Mehmet, and Craig sold four hospitals on this service. Each agreement was slightly different in scope from the others, but they were all a variant of the original value proposition. And they commanded annual fees of $1.5 million to $2 million from each client.

To put this in perspective, the annual revenue of the entire Department of Surgery at Columbia-Presbyterian was $40 million per year. And after all the compensation, benefits, and continuing education expenses for the surgeons, the residents, and the interns, Eric was left with $3 million of discretionary funds. Cardiac surgery accounted for 25% of the department of surgery total—$10 million in revenue and $1 million in discretionary funds.

These four Columbia Heart Hospitals were going to contribute $7 million of annual revenue, and there would be almost no incremental cost required to deliver the services.

We set to work developing a business plan for turning this into a real and sustainable enterprise. We projected that within three years, they would have thirty-five clients that would generate upwards of $60 million in revenue, and would produce 50% to 60% gross margins. We worked with Columbia University and developed licensing agreements for the intellectual property with very favorable terms.

Developing this business, however, involved two key imperatives: First, we needed to create an independent LLC with a capable, experienced CEO. We had Columbia University's agreement in principle to approve this arrangement based on a 15% licensing fee and a 25% ownership stake in the business. Second, we needed Eric, Mehmet, and Craig, who would have an ownership stake in the LLC, to devote 20% of their time to the business, selling and delivering service to clients and serving on the LLC's board of directors.

Remember in the last chapter I said: "Motivating people to embrace change is a tough task. Facts and analysis are nice, but they are rarely enough to cause people to change their ways." This was, unfortunately, the case at Columbia-Presbyterian.

Eric Rose was positioning himself to be appointed Dean of the Medical School. This required his involvement in a variety of personal and professional activities, and, even though this service offering was a game-changer in the industry, he just couldn't bring himself to focus exclusively on this opportunity.

Mehmet Oz was just beginning his television career. He had appeared on *Oprah* several times and had been bitten by the fame bug. It's hard to say that he should have walked away from the *Oprah* gig to focus on this new business opportunity, but for me, it is too bad that he didn't.

Craig Smith had the purest of reasons for shying away from this role. He simply liked to be in the operating room performing surgery. That was, and I assume still is, his passion in life. More power to him, I say.

The Columbia Heart Hospital initiative continued for a few years. But to the best of my knowledge, it no longer exists. I find it interesting that several premier medical centers have moved in this direction in the past five to ten years—namely, Mayo Clinic, Cleveland Clinic, and Johns Hopkins. No one was doing this in 2002.

This was an example of creating a new value proposition from whole cloth. The old one was incapable of providing desired outcomes. So we started over. The work that we did, in partnership with three world-class surgeons, ranks as one of the most interesting intellectual challenges of my professional life.

✳

Too many companies don't give adequate attention to articulating their value proposition. When business leaders say: "I want everybody to be on the same page," this is the page they should be talking about. This is the unifying basis around which the company should be organized and operated. If an employee is faced with a new situation that they must deal with immediately, the company's value proposition should provide them with the guidance they need to do it.

Tony Alibrio at Marriott Food Services had not articulated his value proposition prior to our arrival in 1992. If he had, it would probably have said something about providing outsourced management services to hospitals. After we quantified the considerable value that he did provide, his value proposition said: "Generate superior cost, quality, and satisfaction outcomes for the food service functions of large hospitals by recruiting, training, and developing strong, capable onsite managers and nutritionists; and availing them of the lowest negotiated food prices in the industry, and providing leading-edge productivity management tools."

The Columbia Heart Hospital case study showed a good example of formulating a new value proposition after the old one has become outdated or unsustainable. The new offering was rooted in their core competencies and unique competitive position, and as such, would have been difficult for others to replicate. It also offered growth and margins unavailable in their conventional business.

Articulation of and adherence to a company's value proposition is critical to achieving business success. This is where a business is defined, and, in the words of a former colleague, "the vital few are separated from the trivial many." It is where competitive differentiation should become apparent. It should be specific and constraining. In the words of another colleague, "strategy formulation is mostly concerned with deciding what you are *not* going to do." A well-crafted value proposition does just that.

CHAPTER 8

ALIGN THE ORGANIZATION

I don't want to use the word reorganization. Reorganization to
me is shuffling boxes, moving boxes around. Transformation
means that you're fundamentally changing the way the
organization thinks, the way it responds, the way it leads.
It's a lot more than just playing with boxes.
—Lou Gerstner

Organizations are, by definition, built around an organizing rationale. Historically, most manufacturing-intensive companies have been structured by function: Engineering, Purchasing, Manufacturing, Sales and Marketing, Finance, Human Resources. Distribution, marketing, and service-intensive companies are frequently grouped by geography: U.S., Europe, Asia, Western Region, Central Region. The problem with these organizing rationales is that they are inwardly focused and don't consider customer needs and their associated fulfillment processes.

There are almost always more effective ways to organize a company. The largest and most successful professional service firms—accounting, law, management consulting—are now usually organized by customer within industry; for example, the Citibank client within the Global Financial Services practice. Their major client relationships and their deep industry experience are key competitive differentiators. These often get lost in a geographically-based organization. Other companies organize by product or by capability—Electronic Assembly Division, Electronic Components Division, Software Development Division. This allows engineering to be focused on unique customer needs and keeps the sales force close to the customer.

It is critically important to align the organization with the company's value proposition. As John Kotter said, "Customer-focused visions often fail unless customer-unfocused organizational structures are modified."[12]

THE FIRST TEN MINUTES

Following my relocation to Booz Allen's Atlanta office, more and more of my work took place in service-based industries. As this focus emerged and a distinct practice area began to develop, I decided that I wanted to consult with Marriott Corporation. They were a blue-chip service company, and they were headed by an iconic leader. They were big. They were global. And they were very successful. In the mid-1980s, I met their Senior Vice President of Planning, Tom Curren, and we really hit it off. Tom, it turned out, was a former partner at McKinsey & Company, so there were lots of war stories to be shared.

While Marriott was not a big user of outside consultants, and there was no work forthcoming, I still maintained a relationship with Tom over the years. Often when I was in Washington, D.C. on business, I would meet Tom for dinner. Finally, in 1988, four years after I first met with him, Tom called me to say that one of Marriott's divisions needed some outside help.

I invited my partner Stephen Baum to join me, and we scheduled a meeting with several of the senior operating executives from the hotel group. This was Marriott's core business—the family jewels, so to speak.

They had several concerns about systemic operating cost and resource utilization levels, and about system-wide customer satisfaction rates across the chain. We suggested that we pick one typical hotel and perform an extensive operations and service diagnostic. This would include analysis of their historical performance and their organizational structure, as well as targeted focus groups and market research. They agreed, and approved the proposal that we submitted following our meeting.

As I remember it, they selected a hotel in Newton, Massachusetts, outside of Boston, as being typical in every way: management, demand, revenue, cost, service levels, and ancillary offerings. Stephen and I assembled a team and went to work.

We began with the usual array of internal diagnostic analyses: room, restaurant, and bar revenue; labor, supplies, and overhead costs; demand

---

[12] Kotter, *Leading Change*, 109.

trends and cycles; and organizational structure and spans of control. We also looked at their historical customer satisfaction surveys, although these were so general as to be largely unhelpful.

It wasn't until we began to hold some focus groups that we began to develop some actionable insight. Customers clearly divided themselves into two groups: business travelers and leisure travelers. And the needs and desires of each group were very different from those of the other, in both nature and importance.

We followed this up with some directed market research and came to an interesting set of findings. Business travelers, who made up 80% of this hotel's demand, were most concerned about the following six issues, in rough order of importance:

- Do they have my reservation?
- Is my room available?
- Is it the kind I requested?
- When I get to the room, has it been cleaned?
- Do I have towels?
- Are the TV and phone in working order?

Leisure travelers had a very different list:
- Do they have my reservation?
- Do they have a pool?
- Do they have a bar?
- Do they have a concierge?
- Do they have a game room for the kids?
- Is the restaurant good?

It was striking that most of the major concerns of the business traveler were things that played out virtually upon their arrival, whereas leisure travelers were most concerned about the various offerings that they could avail themselves of during their stay. For the businessman, the hotel was a means to an end. For the vacation traveler, it was an end in itself.

Now, let's look at the hotel's organization chart and see how it matches up with customer needs. First, notice in Exhibit 8 that this is a classical functional organization. Many operations are organized this way to try to maximize utilization and efficiency. But unfortunately, such organizing principles rarely align with the basic value proposition of the business.

Exhibit 8: Marriot Hotel Organization Chart

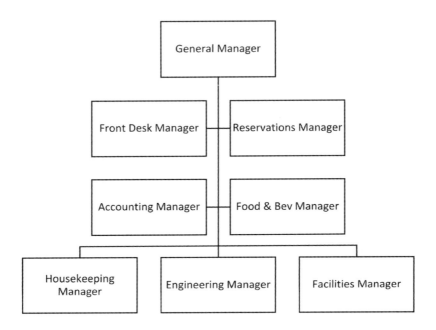

While this specific hotel did not have its own value proposition, if I were to write one, it would say: "Deliver efficient, reliable, high-quality, reasonably-priced lodging to business travelers to the Newton area." Reliability would be defined as consistently meeting the needs and expectations of the hotel's business guests. Note that I have excluded leisure travelers as they only account for 20% of total demand. Pleasing them is important, but it is not a strategic imperative.

Now return to the list of the business travelers' concerns and issues. All six either happen or don't happen within the first ten minutes of a guest's arrival. And four of the department managers have a hand in determining if the customer's expectations are met. No reservation: Reservations Manager; long line, no room, wrong room: Front Desk Manager; cleaning and towels: Housekeeping Manager; TV and phone: Engineering Manager. And as they say, when everyone is accountable, no one is accountable.

We came up with a radically different way to organize and operate the hotel, based on the implicit value proposition. We began by creating a new position: Vice President of the First Ten Minutes. This position would have reporting to it virtually all of the resources required to meet the arriving guest's expectations. Reservations and the front desk were obvious. But we would also divide the housekeeping department into vacated room housekeeping (those being readied for new guests) and carry-over room housekeeping (those being cleaned for returning guests). The standards and time requirements of each of these groups were very different. And combining them into one department inevitably led to compromises and issues.

We also reengineered all the processes connected with the first ten minutes of arrival. The information obtained during reservations was expanded and modified. For example, we added a new question: "What time do you think you will be arriving?" Many guests were flying into Boston on the day of their reservation and they knew their expected hotel arrival time within fifteen minutes.

We insisted that the front desk not ask any question that had been asked, or could have been asked, at the time the reservation was made. The result of this was that there was no need for an arriving guest to check in at the front desk.

Here was how the overall process worked. In the morning, the reservations group would give the arrivals housekeeping supervisor a list of that day's arriving guests, their expected time of arrival, and their preliminary room assignments. The supervisor would then deploy her staff to ensure that the right rooms were ready at the right times. Preliminary room assignments were changed during the day based on late-departing guests or other timing issues.

In the afternoon, the arrivals staff would begin to check arriving guests into the hotel several hours before their expected arrival. They would make key cards and put them into envelopes, with the arriving guest's name clearly printed on the front. They would also note if the guest was a past customer and when they visited last. Then they would personally visit each assigned room to be sure that it had been cleaned and that all was in order.

Later in the afternoon, guests would begin to arrive. An arrivals staff member, dressed in a blazer and a tie, would approach the guest in the middle of the lobby, and a conversation would ensue.

"Excuse me," the staff member would say. "Are you an arriving guest?"

Their luggage was usually a dead giveaway.

"Yes, I am."

"Could I have your name please, sir?"

"Daniel Andrews."

"Just a moment, Mr. Andrews." The arrival staff would then walk to a nearby rack and find the guest's key card envelope.

"Welcome back, Mr. Andrews. We've missed you. You will be staying in Room 603 tonight. It is a king deluxe room overlooking the lake. The elevators are right behind you. Do you need any help with your bags?"

The guest, having bypassed lines, the front desk, and the request for credit cards, would go to the elevator and directly to their room. About five minutes later, the arrival staff member would call the room and ask the guest if everything was to their satisfaction, knowing of course that it had looked perfect three hours before.

The Vice President of the First Ten Minutes, and his reservation, arrivals, and housekeeping staff, had all the resources necessary to ensure a flawless arrival for 99% of the guests. No organizational silos—defined as departments or management groups that do not share information, tools, priorities, and processes with other departments. No competing issues. No diluted authority. The VP had true accountability. The VP's performance review contained measures of customer satisfaction, including precise elements of the arrival process, return customer visits, occupancy, and other measures directed squarely at the effectiveness and impact of the delivery of service during the first ten minutes after a guest arrived.

There were more elements of the reorganization and process reengineering, but this was the most interesting part. We continued to work at the Newton hotel while they tested, tweaked, and piloted this new approach. The results they achieved were amazing. Customer satisfaction scores soared. Labor costs were reduced. Business travelers had a higher propensity to come back, and occupancy rates began to improve significantly.

Executives in the hotel group, including Bill Marriott himself, were excited by this new approach, and created an internal team to oversee its implementation across the Northeastern U.S. region. More important than the actual organizational structure and operating processes themselves was their alignment with their customers' expectations and the hotel's value proposition, whether implicit or explicit.

HUSTLE!

I was privileged to serve on the board of directors of Affiliated Computer Services from 2007 to 2010. ACS was a global provider of outsourced business processes and technology services. Their clients were large and diverse, as were the services they provided. For E-ZPass, for example, they designed, implemented, and managed their information systems; managed all billing and collections processes; and handled their entire customer service operation. E-ZPass was a multi-million-dollar-a-year client. And ACS had many other toll-collecting clients around the world for whom they provided similar services.

For Medicaid, a state-based medical insurance program in the U.S., ACS had service contracts with something like thirty states to receive and process all claims, and to calculate and fulfill all customer payments. Collectively, these clients generated about $300 million in annual revenue.

For other companies, they provided outsourced IT services, whereby ACS supplied all the hardware and software and ran the client's entire IT function. All in, this business generated over $1 billion in recurring annual revenue.

ACS was founded in 1988 by Darwin Deason, who grew the company from one client and a handful of employees to a $6 billion global enterprise with thousands of clients and 75,000 employees. Darwin remained as Executive Chairman until we sold the company to Xerox in 2010 for $8 billion.

I found ACS to be the best managed company I had ever encountered during my thirty-year business career. They delivered real value to their clients, and they did so in a most efficient and effective way. Their success was clearly driven by their ability to out-think, out-manage, and out-hustle their competition.

Their organizational structure facilitated, rather than hindered, their success. I have always thought that Darwin organized the company from the bottom up, not from the top down. The basic organizational building block was the client.

Take the E-ZPass example: a dedicated team of resources provided all of the various services and capabilities required to serve the client. The team was led by a client leader who, because E-ZPass was such a large client, was a very seasoned, senior, and highly compensated individual. He had reporting to him a dedicated team responsible for all the operating systems, another team dedicated to billing and collection, and a third team responsible for the customer service function. ACS resisted all temptation to reorganize these capabilities into functional organizations, even though there would have been synergies and efficiencies available by doing so.

Smaller clients had a part-time client leader and only one or two dedicated staff. Clients were then organized into hierarchical ladders based on the industry being served and the capability being provided. For example, toll collections:

Exhibit 9: ACS Client-Based Organization Structure

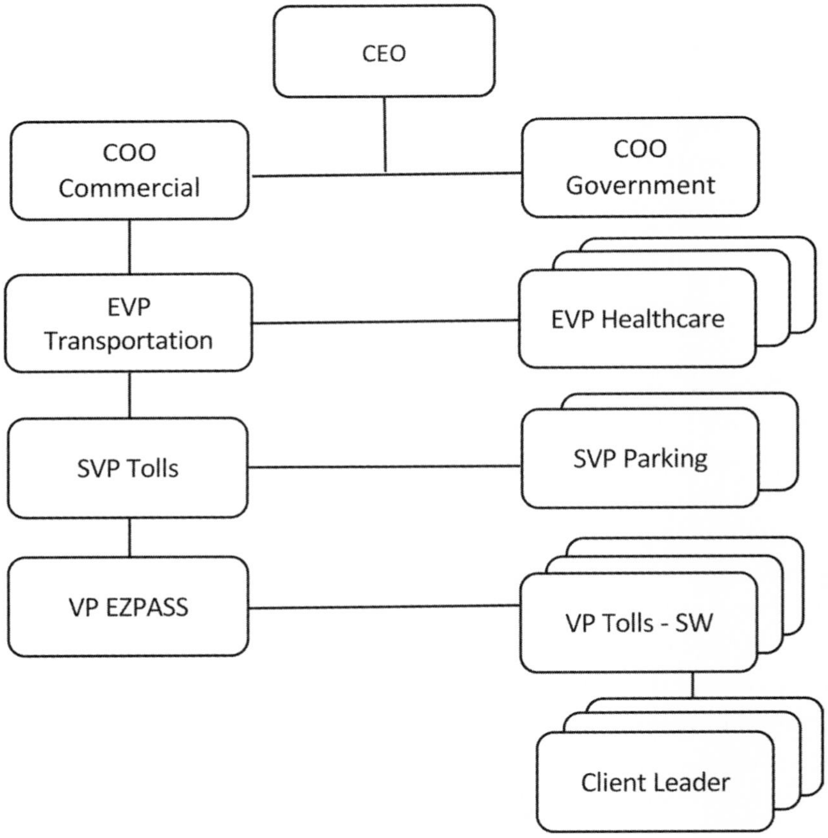

This simplified chart is not far from the actual ACS organization. Seventy-five thousand people were organized into six levels of management. And except for various overhead functions—Legal, HR, Finance—the organization was all structured around clients.

Such a structure—where 95% of the resources required to deliver client work were direct and imbedded in the client team—enabled ACS to measure profitability at the client level. As I said in Chapter 5, I am not a big fan of allocated costs. But where direct costs are over 95% of total costs, what the hell. Management measured each client's profitability every month. And pity the client leader who lost money.

But there were exceptions. Sometimes they lost money by design, such as an investment in a client as part of a business development initiative. Nonetheless, each client that was not profitable was put on a list that was reviewed by all levels of management, including the CEO. And client leaders had seven days to submit a specific plan which explained, first, what happened; second, how they were going to get back in the black; and then, third, how they were going to get back to target profitability. The CEO and COOs were conversant in these plans no matter how big or small the client. They were frequently discussed at board meetings.

Another result of this customer-focused organizational structure was an externally-focused and accountability-based culture. Darwin Deason liked to refer to it as "Hustle!" When I would show up at headquarters for a 7:30 a.m. board meeting, the parking lot would already be nearly full. When I left at 7:30 p.m., the lot was still nearly full. This was, in large part, driven by the strong sense of individual accountability that was imbedded in the corporate culture.

That was reinforced by a compensation system that was perhaps among the best I have ever seen. By plan, every executive at ACS had a base salary pegged to the fifth percentile of peer-based compensation levels: the bottom of the scale. But each also had a target bonus that would reward them at the ninety-fifth percentile or more of their peer group in total compensation. If industry norms for a Fortune 200 Chief Financial Officer were, say, a $500,000 annual salary, with a total cash compensation potential of $800,000, the CFO of ACS might have a base salary of $300,000, but a bonus potential of $700,000, giving him the opportunity to make $1,000,000, or 25% more than his industry peers.

The catch was that in order to qualify for any bonus, the company first had to achieve two financial goals: a 10% year-over-year increase in revenue and a 10% year-over-year increase in net income. If the company fell one dollar short, there were no bonuses paid for the year. Once those goals were met, each executive's group and personal objectives were scored, and bonuses were awarded. Bonuses of two-to-three times base salary were not uncommon. But one year when I was on the board, total company revenue only grew by 8% and no bonuses were paid. Not one dime. Yet I heard no complaining. This was a culture you could cut with a knife.

It's hard to get a functionally- or geographically-organized company to be customer-focused. Such approaches are not inherently bad. It is just that they are so pervasive and often misapplied. It is almost as if the organization is working against itself. Processes inevitably cross several functional silos, which causes them to be more complex and more extensive, with multiple handoffs and opportunities for failure. Worse yet, there is no way to hold anyone except the CEO accountable for the outcome.

The Marriott Hotel case study provides an easy and entertaining example of organizing around a discrete set of customers and their needs. Even though it challenged a lot of conventional thinking about how to organize and operate a hotel, it really did work. And customers were over the moon.

The ACS case study highlights a real success story. As I said, ACS was the best managed company I ever saw. And the biggest enabler of their success was, in my view, their customer-based organization. Resources were efficiently deployed. Utilization of those resources was high. Accountabilities were clear. Problems were quickly brought to light and resolved. And growth initiatives were more typically bottom-up than top-down—that is, they were more likely to grow their presence in existing clients than they were to define and develop new services and new markets. Boy, did it work.

If your organization seems to be constantly fighting itself, and if the company is inwardly focused, try reorganizing around the customer. This often requires a change agent to become a true, eye-poking goad!

CHAPTER 9

STREAMLINE PROCESSES

*When something goes wrong, it's either because there is
too much process, too little process or the wrong process.
Likewise, when something goes right, it's because the
right resources (people or systems) were used at the
right time. What dictates that is again a process.*
—MIHNEA GALETEANU

*Process improvement programs are like teaching people how to fish. Strategy
maps and scorecards teach people where to fish.*
—ROBERT S. KAPLAN

The dictionary defines a *process* as "a systematic series of actions directed to some end."[13] Let's take this definition apart. First, a process is *systematic*. That means it is planned and orderly. In other words, it is methodical. Next, it is a *series*. It has multiple steps, and one step leads to another. The steps follow in succession. There is an order to them. Third, these steps involve *actions*. They are performed or done. They are active, not passive. Finally, they *lead to an end*. There is a purpose to the actions. They are performed to accomplish something specific.

Businesses run on processes. They are the way that everything gets done inside a company. Without a purchasing process, or multiple purchasing processes, nothing would ever be bought. Without a recruiting process, no one would ever be hired. Without a payroll process, employees would never be paid. The payroll process may be complicated and involve several people,

---

[13] "process," Dictionary.com, 2017, accessed June 2017, www.dictionary.com.

a set of policies, and interactions with a sophisticated computer system. Or the CEO may just go to the bank, get some cash, and walk the halls handing out hundred-dollar bills. Either way, there is a payroll process.

The reason for this perhaps silly example is to emphasize that processes are the basic way that everything gets done in a company. And as such, they are usually a rich source of operational and customer satisfaction improvements in the achieved outcomes of an enterprise.

Because of this, they should be a primary focus of any change effort. Start with basic business processes. Understand them, map them, measure compliance with them, time them, and understand the resources required to perform them. They will lead you to the performance leverage that you seek.

A DAY IN THE LIFE OF A LETTUCE

In 1989, I received a call from Don Tomasso, CEO of the fast food chain Roy Rogers. Marriott Corporation started Roy's in 1968, and by 1989, they had 648 stores throughout the Mid-Atlantic and Northeastern U.S. Don was concerned about the performance of the business. He knew that the efficiency and effectiveness of his store operations was declining. Note: In the fast food industry, a restaurant is called a store.

Don and I met in his office in Bethesda, Maryland and talked through his concerns. As the industry had become more price competitive in the 1980s, Roy Rogers' margins had been trending down. Productivity had stayed constant, and thus, labor cost increases could not be offset by price increases.

I reviewed my background and experience, and explained the way I would approach the work and the outcomes I expected to see. Don asked for a proposal. Within a week, I wrote a proposal and met with him to review it. After some questions and discussion, he approved the assignment.

I assembled a team of three full-time service operations staff, and we went to work. We collected a load of historical data—productivity, labor rates, quality, demand, revenue, cost—and set about analyzing it.

Then we selected four stores in the D.C. area to study in depth. We spent several weeks at each one and closely observed operations. We watched the staff take orders, cook burgers, fry fries, and everything else that they do in any fast food restaurant.

I clearly remember standing out of the way at one store during the lunchtime rush. Every few minutes, one of the employees would bump into me, or another employee, as they were hurrying by. I started to pay closer attention to this, and discovered that they were generally going to the walk-in cooler or the freezer in the back of the store to retrieve cold or frozen food—hamburger patties, raw french fries, lettuce, tomatoes, cheese—you get the idea. I started to keep track of the frequency and duration of this activity, and concluded that each worker spent about 15% of their time walking from one place to another.

We bored in on this issue and spent considerable time documenting processes and work flows at each store. It became increasingly clear that one of the factors impeding labor efficiency was the basic store layout, in which there was a very large refrigeration unit at the rear of the store. One half of it was a freezer; the other half was a cooler. Food was moved in and out of the freezer and cooler all day long.

Just for fun, I asked the team to investigate the process by which lettuce moved from the cooler in Roy Rogers' regional food distribution center to the individual Roy's store, and ultimately onto the customer's cheeseburger.

Bulk quantities of lettuce were stored in a large crate in a cooler at the Roy's distribution center. In the middle of the night, based on a replenishment order from a specific Roy's store, a stock picker would pick some number of these heads of lettuce and put them into a shipping bin. This bin would be moved to the shipping staging area where the store's order would be staged for several hours. At 7:00 a.m., the complete order would be loaded onto a refrigerated delivery truck, along with the orders for five other stores. By 7:45, the truck was ready to roll.

The delivery truck would arrive at our store at about 11:30 every morning. Since this was the start of the lunchtime rush, the order was taken off the truck and put into the receiving staging area at the rear of the store. Everything sat there until the rush was over at 1:30 p.m. Then someone was assigned to put everything away. The lettuce was then moved into the freezer, because the cooler was always too full.

Sometime in the afternoon, the manager would ask an employee to go and shred the lettuce. The employee would remove ten or twelve heads from the freezer and take them to a prep table in the back of the store, shred the lettuce using an electric shredding machine, put the shredded lettuce into plastic bags, put the bags into a different bin, and move the bin into the cooler.

Prior to the dinner rush, the manager would instruct the staff to restock the food assembly stations in the kitchen, and someone would get a bin of shredded lettuce and fill up the containers on the assembly line. There it would sit until it was used to make a sandwich, presumably during the dinner demand period.

I asked the team to put together an attention-grabbing exhibit that demonstrated how the lettuce passed from temperature zone to temperature zone throughout the day. Their handiwork is shown in Exhibit 10.

Exhibit 10: A Day in the Life of a Lettuce

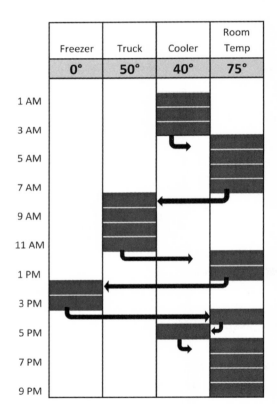

When we presented this to Don Tomasso and his management team, Don's response was priceless: "No wonder this stuff tastes so bad!"

Don did institute changes in the process to improve the quality of their product. He instructed store managers to move arriving cold foods directly into the cooler on arrival, and he decreased the amount of assembly station resupply while increasing its frequency. Have you noticed the improved taste of a Roy Rogers burger?

Admittedly, this example did little to contribute to improving Roy's operating margins by 20%. But process mapping such as this was a key element of the diagnostic analysis that led to the structural improvements which *did* result in higher margins.

There are much richer and more substantive examples of process simplification shown in other chapters. But, however simple, this one has always been a favorite of mine, because it illustrates so clearly how a picture is worth a thousand words, and it does so in a memorable way.

WELCOME BACK!

In Chapter 8, I told of our work at a Marriott Hotel, and how we reorganized key operations within the hotel around a set of customer expectations. I briefly touched on the check-in process, but did not explore it in detail. This case study will do that. I chose this example not because it was the most significant or impactful of my career, but because it is one that anyone who has ever checked into a hotel can appreciate.

We began our work by thoroughly understanding the check-in process, based on observations and interviews. Then we drew a typical process flow chart. I'll share the flow chart in Exhibit 11 but will present it in a novel way. I will go beyond the usual approach of tersely describing a work step and showing it inside a box that is linked to the preceding and following work steps. Instead, I'll describe the process by providing the conversation that occurred between the front desk clerk and the arriving guest, and I will add my reaction and critique in italics.

This process took over ten minutes to complete, including the two interruptions. It was frustrating, and at times, caused apprehension for the customer: Did they lose my reservation? Will I get my king bed? Worst of all, it solicited no additional information from the customer beyond that which he had provided when making his reservation.

Our reorganizational work led us to redesign this process. We established one inviolate rule: You could not ask the customer for any information that you had learned, or could have learned, during the reservation process.

Poof! The entire process disappeared except for two questions: "Are you checking in?" and "Could I have your name please?" That led us to

Exhibit 11: Marriott Hotel Check-In Process

"Hello, welcome to Marriott. Are you checking in?"

"Yes."
No, I'm actually here to refinance my house.

"Could I have your name, please?
"Yes. It's Daniel Andrews."

Desk phone rings. Clerk answers it.

"Front desk. How may I assist you?" Pause. "Yes, the restaurant is open until 10 PM." Pause. "You're welcome. Have a nice evening." Pause. "Goodbye."

Just when we were starting to make progress.

Clerk accesses data base and locates the reservation.

"Here you are. I see that you will be staying for two nights and requested an executive king room."

"Yes."
Just like I told 'em when I made my reservation!

"Is this your first visit to our hotel?"

"No, I've been here twice a month for the past year."

It's always nice to be remembered.

"Well, welcome back. Could you please confirm your home address?

"1214 Elm Street, Lima Ohio."

It's the same one I gave them when I made my reservation, and the same one that I gave you last week!

"Thank you. Could I have a credit card?"

"Here you are," as the credit card is handed over.

Once again, it's the same one I gave them when I made my reservation and the same one I gave you last week!

"Excuse me just a minute."

Clerk disappears into the back room and returns three minutes later.

"Sorry about that."

Where on earth did she go?

"Okay," she says as my credit card is returned. "I have you in Room 603."

"Is it an executive king?"

"I'm sorry. We don't have any king beds available. It's an executive double."

Maybe I should try that hotel down the street!

"How many keys do you need?"

"One"

Clerk copies one key, puts it in an envelope, writes my room number on it, and hands it to me.

"Elevator is behind you on the right. Thank you."

Maybe I will try that hotel down the street!

blow up the entire front desk check-in process and handle arrivals as was described in Chapter 8: Arrival housekeeping staff prioritizes room cleaning based on expected guest arrival time; arrivals staff checks in the guest prior to their arrival and confirms the readiness of the room; arrival staff greets arriving guests, asks for their name, gives them their key, and asks if they need any assistance.

We also changed the check-out process, although this was pretty simple. Up until this time, guests were forced to appear at the front desk to check out. We decided to have the overnight staff check out departing guests at 4 a.m., and slide their receipt under their room doors. That way, only guests with issues would need to stop at the front desk. Believe it or not, this was a novel idea in 1988.

In addition to thrilling every business traveler to whom we spoke, these innovative approaches had another major benefit: cost reduction. When we began our work, the front desk was staffed with ten full-time equivalents each day from Monday to Friday. At peak times, the staff was overloaded and customers were forced to wait. But the changes that we implemented dramatically smoothed out the work load. The one overnight employee, who had historically been only 25% utilized, was now productively engaged 75% of the time. Similarly, the day staff no longer had to deal with check-out volumes in the morning and had time to check in most arriving guests in the afternoon. In total, the new processes enabled us to cut front desk staff by 30% while simultaneously improving customer satisfaction.

*

Process flow charts typically look like the X-ray flow chart from Chapter 5. I purposely chose the case studies in this chapter to showcase unconventional approaches to process mapping. Hopefully, this will broaden your thinking about processes and process reengineering.

The Roy Rogers' case study about a day in the life of a lettuce was meant to demonstrate one way to think about a series of steps or movements over a given period of time. It also showed an example of creatively presenting facts and analysis so as to memorably engage your audience. Had I just presented the facts and avoided the humor, it is likely that management would not have engaged and would have taken no action. As it was, they did both.

The Marriott Hotel check-in process was described in a conversational way so that anyone who has ever checked into a hotel could relate. Again, this made a big impression on the client and led them, at least in this region, to eliminate the front desk check-in process.

If you've been paying close attention, you should have noticed that this is the second case study based on the work we did for Marriott hotels: the first dealt with organizational structure; this one dealt with process reengineering. Such points of leverage often are not isolated from one another, but work together synergistically.

In my experience, there is considerable performance improvement leverage contained in basic process improvement. Be it cost reduction, lead time reduction, or customer satisfaction improvement that you seek, start with processes. Observe them. Understand them. Flow-chart them. Time-phase them. And cost them. And then follow your instincts and your common sense.

Bob Kaplan, a Professor Emeritus at Harvard Business School, who was the dean of the business school at Carnegie Mellon University while I was attending graduate school there, put it this way: "Consistent alignment of capabilities and internal processes with the customer value proposition is the core of any strategy execution."

CHAPTER 10

INCREASE UTILIZATION

Our biggest cost is not power, or servers, or people. It's lack of utilization.
It dominates all other costs.
—JEFF BEZOS

Companies use assets to create and deliver a product or service. These may be capital assets or human assets. The assets used in this process form the basis of the value created by the company, whether the product or service is priced by the pound or the hour or the unit. And the financial viability of the company is almost always driven by the utilization of these assets.

The dictionary defines *utilization* as "to make practical or worthwhile use of."[14] In a business context, utilization refers to the percentage of time that assets and resources are actually engaged in making a product or delivering a service, and thereby generating revenue. For example, in a machine shop during an eight-hour shift, if a lathe sits idle for one hour, is being set up for one hour, and is cranking out parts for six hours, the lathe is 75% utilized. The same is true of an accountant who spends six hours working on tax returns and two hours in a training class. She is 75% utilized.

It is vital that companies manage the utilization of their assets, be they equipment or people. For most, it is the determining factor in their success and sustainability.

---

[14] "utilization," Dictionary.com, 2017, accessed June 2017, www.dictionary.com.

GET OFF THE BEACH!

Professional service firms are perhaps the organizations that are most dependent on effective resource utilization. Low staff utilization will destine them to fail. Adequate staff utilization will destine them to mediocrity. High staff utilization will fuel growth, profitability, and big bonuses.

This lesson was made real when I joined Booz Allen Hamilton in 1978. It was made clear that one of the primary indicators of my performance and promise would be my individual billability, i.e., the percentage of a forty-hour work week that I was able to bill to a paying client; in other words, my utilization. If I was capable, I would be in demand and my billability would increase. If I was lacking, demand for my involvement would fall off, and my billability would go down.

The target billability for Associates was 95%. As one was promoted and moved up the ladder, these targets came down, first to 85%, then to 75%. But even Senior Partners had a billability target of 50%. One always spent the unbillable portion of one's time on productive activities: training, business development, selling. But these activities did not generate revenue and, as such, were considered a means to the end: getting billable. Anyone who was unbillable was termed to be "on the beach," as in relaxing by the seashore instead of working. You did not want to be on the beach.

At Booz Allen, we charged for our consulting services by the hour. Our hourly rate was a set multiple of our base compensation. Using our multiple of 5.1, a staff member having an annual salary of $100,000 would be billed to a client at $245 per hour—$100,000 times 5.1 equals $510,000, which was then divided by the 2080 standard work hours in a year to arrive at $245.19 per hour.

The difference between the staff member's revenue generation and their base compensation was not pure profit. It went to pay for employee benefits, offices, support staff, and a variety of other necessary expenses. Plus, it had to fund underutilization. That said, our pre-tax profit margins were usually about 40%. These were used to fund various investments, and pay partner bonuses.

The entire professional staff at Booz Allen averaged 85% billability in most years. When an office or a practice had average billability greater than 88% over three months, they would hire additional staff. And when their billability fell to 82% during any three-month period, they would aggressively terminate marginal performers.

Staff utilization was, without question, the primary determinant of the firm's profitability and resulting partner bonuses. As such, it was rigorously managed on a daily basis.

✳

Contrast this environment with the one I found when I began working with another professional service firm in 1993. Burson-Marsteller was, at the time, the largest public relations and marketing communications firm in the world, with seventy-five offices in forty-five countries. They were the largest subsidiary of advertising giant Young & Rubicam.

I was retained to assist them on a variety of issues. But the most important one was to help them improve their financial performance; specifically, their profit margins. For several years, Burson had woefully under-performed relative to both plans and expectations. Their overall profit margin was 2%. In the U.S., it was 5%, and their offices in the rest of the world were basically break-even. Y&R expected this situation to be remedied toot sweet.

Given that Burson was a professional services firm that sold their capabilities to clients on an hourly basis, the first statistic that I tried to look at was client staff billability. Imagine my surprise when I discovered that staff billability wasn't even measured, let alone reported. No wonder their profits were in the tank.

I knew that the staff had to submit weekly time sheets to enable clients to be billed for services rendered. But it seemed that no one had ever bothered to accumulate this data to determine or manage client staff utilization.

I went to the IT Department to see what I could find. Sure enough, they had data on all U.S. staff members' time sheets going back for a year. I asked them to cobble together a one-off report that calculated the total staff billability for the past twelve months based on the actual hours charged to actual clients by week and by staff member. A week later, I had the results.

Total billability of the U.S. client staff for the preceding twelve months was 48%. That's right, 48%. No wonder they weren't making any money. The old adage holds: if you don't measure it, you can't manage it.

The entire senior management team was astounded by this fact. And they readily agreed that the European, Asian, and Latin American regions would fare worse, once we had the data to measure them. As a group, we began to look at the root causes for this apparently systemic problem.

First, it seemed that a lot of the problem was caused by simply not paying attention. This was not an area on which management focused and there were no consequences for poor billability. This was undoubtedly compounded by the apprehension client leaders felt when sending an invoice to a client that reflected these billed hours. There was an obvious lack of confidence among client leaders throughout the U.S. that the firm was providing value commensurate with their fees.

Second, it also seemed clear that the U.S. business was significantly overstaffed. There were simply too many staff members competing for too few client assignments. The data suggested that each level of the organization, from Associate to Managing Director, was overstaffed.

Third, while not readily provable, it made sense that the firm was selling too many small engagements. If a Managing Director sold a client assignment for $250,000 that required four full-time staff for three months, there would be a long period of 100% billability for that staff. On the other hand, if the assignment were for $25,000 and required four part-time staff for one month, there would be a lot of slippage in their individual billability, due to the continual starting and stopping of work.

We began to attack these three issues in the U.S. first. Burson reduced their U.S. client staff by 15%. This was done strictly by merit and across all organizational levels. In addition to reducing cost, this move raised the average talent level and the professional capability of the remaining staff appreciably.

At the same time, we developed a management report which showed staff billability, and sliced and diced the numbers by client, practice area, position, and office; and we disseminated this information to every manager and client leader every week. Management began to follow up with offices and practices that had low billability.

We also developed a new policy whereby any proposed client assignment priced at $50,000 or less required the sign-off of the U.S. CEO to move forward. There was a lot of grousing, but this policy was slowly accepted and acted upon.

In the first year, Burson was able to increase U.S. margins to 12%. And by 1998, when I was serving as Chief Financial Officer, the U.S. business was routinely generating 28% to 30% margins. This was goading at its best. The rest of the world was slow to follow because of the culture that permeated most of the European and Asian offices. Were it not for the need to have a truly global network of capabilities, I would have begun to close various offices outside of the U.S.

By 2000, when we sold Y&R to The WPP Group, total profit margins for Burson-Marsteller were about 12%. This represented a profit improvement of more than $30 million per year. And it was all driven by staff utilization.

HUB & SPOKE

The College Board is an American not-for-profit organization that was formed in December 1899 to expand access to higher education. Membership in the College Board includes more than 6,000 schools, colleges, universities, and other educational organizations. The College Board contracts with the Educational Testing Service (ETS) to develop and administer standardized tests as part of the college admissions process. They are best known for developing and administering the SAT, PSAT, and Advanced Placement tests that all high school juniors and seniors know so well.

In the mid-1980s, the College Board and ETS had problems with the administration of their largest program. The SAT test was, and still is, typically offered on the first Saturday of October, December, March, and May. Candidates register online at the College Board's website, by mail, or by telephone, at least three weeks before the test date. In 2013/2014, the SAT was administered to 1.67 million high school students.[15]

In 1984, their problem had to do with the utilization rates of the various centers around the country in which the tests were administered. These centers were located at local high schools, community colleges, and universities in the area. It was not uncommon for there to be 4,000 different locations across the country for any given test. Each of these centers had a set of fixed costs: center manager, proctors, security, janitorial, and often, a facility fee.

A center might be created to administer the test to, say, 150 students—six rooms and proctors of twenty-five students each. These arrangements and costs had to be scheduled, and agreed upon with the locations and the

---

[15] "2014 College Board Results: SAT," Collegeboard.org, accessed May 2017, www.collegeboard.org/program-results/2014/sat.

participants, months in advance. But the students could register up to three weeks before the exam date. Thus, the problem: the utilization rates of individual centers drove the relative impact of fixed costs on the economics of test administration.

In this example, if 150 students showed up for the test, the center was 100% utilized and the administration cost per test was very low. But if only 75 students showed up, the resulting 50% utilization rate caused average administration costs to double. Ouch!

Over the three previous years, the average center utilization rates had ranged from 40% to 100%, with an average of 73%. The College Board wanted to reduce the number of testing sites to increase average center utilization, and commensurately reduce unit administration costs. That was our challenge.

We dove into the data and tried to understand test center utilization. What were the trends? Did different regions of the country trend differently? How about cities? Could you correlate center utilization with any exogenous factors?

Nothing that we tried yielded any results. Demand for a center seemed to be, within a given range, truly independent of possible predictive factors, such as test month, historical demand, or demographically similar test centers. It began to look like we were going to need to either close or radically downsize centers to achieve any cost savings.

We started to develop lists of potential closures based on the most underutilized centers over time. Unfortunately, when we analyzed those centers, some of them had exam dates where they had been 100% utilized. And others were geographically isolated, the next-nearest center being one hundred miles away.

Then we took another look at the data, this time focusing on urban areas, not test center locations. Of course, the demand patterns across periods began to level out. Exhibit 12 shows what we found in the centers in a medium-sized metropolitan area over the previous three years.

Note that the average center utilization over these three years was 85%, much improved over the national average of 73%. But the telling statistics were the standard deviations: single centers ranged from 23.5 to 31.8, whereas the entire region was only 11.6. This was the exploitable finding. Demand at the center level varied dramatically from exam to exam. But regional demand was almost three times more consistent.

Exhibit 12: SAT Metro Testing Centers

	East HS	West HS	South HS	North HS	Total
Capacity	250	250	250	250	1000
10/82	240	200	190	250	880
12/82	210	220	190	230	850
3/83	160	240	240	220	860
5/83	230	250	220	150	850
10/83	200	240	235	170	845
12/83	190	220	185	250	845
3/84	250	180	210	200	840
5/84	250	175	225	210	860
10/84	180	240	180	235	835
12/84	210	240	230	180	860
3/85	155	250	240	200	845
5/85	235	195	180	250	860
Average	209	221	210	212	853
Utilization	84%	88%	84%	85%	85%
Std. Dev.	31.7	25.9	23.5	31.8	11.6

We didn't need to close any centers; we simply needed to employ a hub-and-spoke approach, whereby most centers were sized to achieve a very high utilization rate at every exam, and one center in each geographical area was sized to absorb any overflow from sold out centers. Here are the demand and utilization statistics for the same metropolitan area after we applied the new approach.

Exhibit 13 shows that standard deviation of demand dropped by over 50% at the spoke centers. This allowed their utilization to be increased from about 85% to over 95%. And the hub center (North High School) was still able to achieve a utilization rate of 89%, higher than any of the centers had achieved in the past. Overall utilization for the metro area increased from 85% to 94%, which, enabled an 11% reduction in center variable costs.

Exhibit 13: Adjusted SAT Metro Testing Centers

	East HS	West HS	South HS	North HS	Total
Capacity	200	220	200	290	910
10/82	200	200	190	290	880
12/82	200	220	190	240	850
3/83	160	220	200	280	860
5/83	200	220	200	230	850
10/83	200	220	200	225	845
12/83	190	220	185	250	845
3/84	200	180	200	260	840
5/84	200	175	200	285	860
10/84	180	220	180	255	835
12/84	200	220	200	240	860
3/85	155	220	200	270	845
5/85	200	195	180	285	860
Average	190	209	194	259	853
Utilization	95%	95%	97%	89%	94%
Std. Dev.	18.8	16.4	7.9	21.7	11.6

The metro regions had to be reasonably limited in area so that students wouldn't be greatly inconvenienced. But this was easy to do in most geographies. When registrations at a "spoke" test center reached capacity, new registrants were simply directed to the "hub" center. Students might then have to drive ten miles instead of three miles to a testing center.

We applied this methodology to metropolitan areas throughout the U.S. and it yielded dramatic results. Utilization across the system rose by 12% (nine percentage points). Variable operating costs were reduced by 15%. And best of all, not one student was turned away, nor was anyone inconvenienced more than having to drive a few extra miles to the testing center.

We also recommended that ETS create a position titled Center Utilization Manager, whose job it would be to regularly update demand history and reconfigure or resize testing centers based on the analysis of local and regional demand variability. This should, we said, become an ongoing process if the anticipated benefits were to be sustained. We also pointed out that a similar methodology might be used on other testing programs offered by ETS and The College Board. The client enthusiastically accepted our findings and recommendations and began to implement them immediately.

I agree with Jeff Bezos, founder and CEO of Amazon. The cost of asset and resource underutilization dominates all other costs. As we saw in the Burson-Marsteller case study, staff utilization is the primary driver of profits, cash flow, and executive bonuses at a professional service firm. At Burson, the difference between 50% staff utilization and 80% staff utilization was about thirty margin points, or no executive bonuses versus big executive bonuses.

Utilization was also the key driver of per test operating costs for ETS and The College Board as they administered the SAT test. To be successful, they needed a structural approach that satisfied virtually all demand without incurring under-utilization cost penalties. The hub-and-spoke approach did just that.

The key lessons here are that (1) increased utilization is often the key to sustainable profit improvement, (2) you get what you measure, and (3) out-of-the-box thinking is often required to crack the code. But usually, when structural changes are made to organizations, deployment strategies, and processes in order to increase utilization, the resulting cost reductions and service enhancements are almost always sustainable.

CHAPTER 11

REDUCE COMPLEXITY

"Nature is pleased with simplicity. And Nature is no dummy."
—ISAAC NEWTON

Complexity is pervasive in our lives. Just consider your smart phone; the features and functionality are mind-boggling. Yes, dedicated users can easily master it; but there is no denying that it is complex. Similarly, most companies are forced to deal with an incredible amount of complexity in one way or another. Maybe it is in their product design or their manufacturing processes. Maybe it is in the number of products that they offer for sale. Maybe it is in their sales or distribution processes. But it is almost always present. And it usually has a dramatic impact on costs.

Two industries that deal with an inordinate amount of complexity are the automotive industry and the retail industry. I was privileged to work with some of the biggest players in these industries and to address head on the issue of cost driven by unnecessary or pervasive complexity.

THERE'S A REASON THEY CALL IT A STORE

Have you ever wondered why a bricks-and-mortar retail outlet is called a store? Why isn't it called a sell? I know why this is true. It's because the true mission of most retail outlets is to store stuff, not to sell it. Read on.

In 1982, I won a major supply chain management assignment at Service Merchandise Corporation in Nashville, Tennessee. They were one of the first catalog showroom retailers, offering fine jewelry, toys, sporting goods, and electronics in a unique retail environment. Service Merchandise was known for its unusual shopping experience, which emphasized the catalog, even within the showrooms. I described their approach in detail in Chapter 5.

Our assignment was to critically assess their existing supply chain—purchasing, merchandising, warehousing, distribution, and inventory management—and identify inefficiencies and areas for potential improvement.

We began our work by thoroughly understanding and documenting the existing supply chain. In an overly-simplified way, here is how it worked. The merchandising group would decide that they wanted to offer a new item, say a Black & Decker drill. They would decide on an order quantity, say 4,000, to be delivered by October 1 in time for the holiday shopping season. The buyer would then meet with a Black & Decker sales rep to negotiate price and terms for the order. They always tried to get the supplier to pay for shipping costs and forced them to accept a retail concept called "dating," whereby the supplier would deliver the goods by October 1, but would not require payment until December 31. That way, Service Merchandise theoretically wouldn't pay for merchandise until after they had sold it.

Suppliers ultimately agreed to such terms, although obviously, they took the additional costs for shipping and deferred billing into consideration when they set the unit prices. In our example, Black & Decker would ship the drills as promised to five different Service Merchandise distribution centers (DCs). Shortly thereafter, each DC would ship perhaps ten drills to each store in its region, and would hold back maybe two hundred at the DC for back-up stock.

Each store would then sell the drills and reorder from the DC as appropriate. When it was time to reorder from Black & Decker, the merchandising buyer would forecast demand and determine an optimal order quantity. Then she would ensure that such a purchase fell within the constraints of their open-to-buy system. This system, which was common in the retail industry, constrained buyers from purchasing more merchandise than was sold over a rolling three-month period. This was an illogical process that stopped buyers from reordering hot-selling merchandise to compensate for slow-moving inventory that they had over-bought in the past.

Much of our work involved disabusing Service Merchandise of their price negotiating strategies and their open-to-buy policies. This was goadism at its finest. We demonstrated that with data and analysis, they could negotiate better prices from their suppliers if they strove for the lowest possible net unit cost, and paid for shipping and capital costs themselves—i.e., they paid for merchandise when it was received. As a multi-billion-dollar enterprise, Service Merchandise could almost always get lower capital costs than their smaller suppliers. Finally, an improved forecasting system and more frequent ordering would allow inventory levels to be managed more tightly and make open-to-buy systems unnecessary.

The most meaningful part of our supply chain work, however, centered on trying to cope with their demand patterns. Almost all retailers deal with extraordinary complexity arising from the large number of SKUs (stock keeping units) that are carried at a store. It is usually many tens of thousands of discrete items. Wal-Mart reportedly stocks over 140,000 different items at its supercenters.

Here is an unbelievable nugget of data from 1983: seventy-three percent of Service Merchandise's SKUs had historical demand of less than one per store per month. We were shocked when we discovered this information. Here is a chart that shows the relative demand of SKUs at the store level over a twelve-month period:

Exhibit 14: Demand Per Store Per Month

% of All SKUs	Quantity
73%	<1
12%	1-3
8%	4-9
3%	10-25
2%	25-100
1%	100-500
<1%	>500

This meant that the entire supply chain basically existed to support sales levels of ones and twos at the store level, for tens of thousands of items.

Remember the Black & Decker drill. There was a good chance that if they sent ten drills to each location, each store would have over a year's worth of inventory. Not good. The issue was not so much double handling of merchandise and lost inventory, as we will see in another retail example. It was simply that Service Merchandise was carrying too much inventory. We set about trying to cut inventory in half and improve inventory turns from three to six. (Turns are the number of times inventory is sold or used in a given time period, usually a year.)

First, we segmented the SKUs into two groups: high demand, which we defined as having a store-level demand greater than five units per month, the point at which demand became statistically significant and therefore forecastable. About 15% of the SKUs fell into this category. Conventional inventory control tools could be used to manage demand, fulfillment, and inventory for this group.

Then we turned our attention to the SKUs with demand of less than five per store per month, 85% of which had demand of less than one per store per month. These demand levels were not statistically forecastable. Nor were there any standard inventory management approaches for dealing with such low-demand items. Demand for these items was simply not statistically significant at the store level. We came up with a concept called one-to-show and one-to-go, meaning that each store would have one of an item on display, and another in the warehouse. When one of these items was sold, another would be shipped from the regional DC.

This, and other initiatives, enabled Service Merchandise to save over $75 million in supply chain costs every year. Over 80% of the savings came from reduced inventory carrying costs. Perhaps even more significantly, the number of store-level stock-outs dropped by over 40%. Complexity, in the form of broad consumer choices, is costly. Again, there is a reason they call it a store.

A few years later, we did a similar supply chain management assignment for Target Stores. They had built a distribution system that was a hallmark of efficiency. Full truckloads were shipped to each store perhaps three times a week. Full case packs were shipped on most items. The five regional warehouses worked two shifts and standard forty-hour weeks with no overtime. Selective use of automation made each warehouse a very efficient operation. It would have been hard to wring any cost savings out of this distribution system.

Unfortunately, Target had demand patterns that were like those of Service Merchandise. Forty-eight percent their SKUs had demand of less than one unit per store per month. Only 25% of the SKUs had statistically significant demand of greater than five units per store per month.

The impact of low relative demand rates and a high-volume distribution operation collided at the store. If a store was selling two bottles per month of a certain shampoo, and the warehouse was sending them a case pack of twenty-four bottles whenever they needed replenishment, imagine how the store was forced to respond. First, they had a twelve-month inventory of this specific SKU if they started with zero; more likely, they started with three or four.

Second, they had to bring the case to the sales floor, replenish one or two empty spaces on the shelf, and return the rest of the carton to the back room, which was not designed to be a warehouse. Often merchandise was misplaced and lost. And store labor was regularly engaged in trying to locate merchandise and replenish store shelves on a onesy-twosy basis. Stock clerks may have had to handle our case of shampoo fifteen times before it was empty.

The net effect was that the cost of the inefficiencies at the store level, when multiplied by the number of stores in the chain, dwarfed any savings generated by an efficient distribution system. Thus, distribution was charged with restructuring their operations to make them consistent with the realities of store-level demand and the resulting store operations. The goal was to make the stores efficient. Distribution needed to replenish the stores daily, and replace the exact sales quantities. If a store sold two bottles of shampoo, the warehouse needed to send two bottles of shampoo. And if the stores were open seven days a week, so were the warehouses. You get the idea.

I thought that the VP of Distribution was going to jump out of his skin when we presented our conclusions and recommendations. He had to learn that his job was to make the stores operate efficiently, even if this resulted in his operations incurring significant inefficiencies. The warehouses had to be transformed from capital-intensive, full-case operations to labor-intensive, break-pack operations. This change reduced the cost and complexity of having to operate store backrooms—mini-warehouses, in effect—across the entire chain by moving storage and handling functions upstream to a few warehouses.

It took Target Stores several years to complete this transformation. At that time, the President, Ken Woodrow, who had been our original client when he was the CFO, tracked me down and called me. "Well, Kurt," he said, "it took us four years, but we have now fully implemented your recommendations. I'm happy to report that things are running smoothly and we are realizing all the benefits that you projected. Nice work and thanks."

Ken went on to say that transformation often requires the cooperation of third parties; in this case, the manufacturers of the products sold at Target, who needed to be encouraged, educated, and convinced that increased cost on their end—like reducing case pack size—will pay dividends. This was a big part of the reason, he said, that it took several years to fully implement the transformation.

✳

The retail industry demonstrates one aspect of the cost of complexity: that of having thousands of SKUs with very low demand. The resulting inventory carrying costs, handling costs, and inventory shrinkage can be profound. That said, complexity costs are often more significant in manufacturing industries.

<h2 style="text-align:center">10[9]</h2>

I led two related assignments at General Motors in 1985. Our client was George Peables, the CEO of GM Canada. He was responsible for all GM activity in Canada: sales, marketing, and manufacturing. Based on the suggestion of a colleague of his, Mr. Peables called me one afternoon and asked me to visit him. When we met the following week, he told me that he was very conflicted about the supposed cost of complexity in automotive manufacturing. He recognized that there had to be some cost penalty involved with offering a variety of drive train options, trim options, and free-standing options. He said that his manufacturing people were always complaining about this. On the other hand, his sales and marketing people were of a mind that customers demanded choices when making such a sizable purchase, and that any attempt to reduce consumer choice would result in lost revenue.

Out of frustration, he demanded that the captain seat option in one of their van models be eliminated. Over the past year, he said, there had only been 350 vehicles equipped with this option, so he thought that the risk would be low. When he then went to the manufacturing VP and asked how much cost-savings there would be in the assembly plant, he was told "none."

"How can this be?" he asked me. "If product complexity drives manufacturing costs, and I reduce that complexity, how can it be that there are no savings to be had?"

I had thought a lot about the impact of complexity on a manufacturing environment, and had some thoughts about the nature of these costs.

"It would make sense that complexity might have a modest impact on cost if it is relatively contained," I offered. "But then as processes get more complicated and variable, costs might rise dramatically until they reached a point where further complexity has an insignificant impact. Maybe that's what is happening here."

I rose and walked over to the whiteboard that was hanging on his wall, and drew the graph shown in Exhibit 15.

Exhibit 15: Hypothesized Cost of Complexity

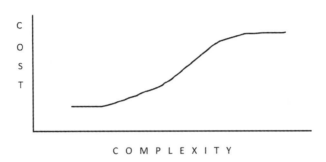

George and I discussed this idea and its possible implications for an hour. Then he said: "I want to hire you to draw that curve."

I said that I would talk with some of my partners and promised a proposal within ten days. I returned to my office and reached out to my colleague Steve Griffiths, and together we hammered out an approach to determine the cost of complexity in the auto industry.

First, we had to agree on a definition of complexity as experienced by the manufacturing function. We settled on build configurations, i.e., the number of unique ways that the car could be assembled, trimmed, and painted. And we selected the Chevy Monte Carlo, which was assembled at GM Canada's Oshawa plant, to be our guinea pig. Based upon the available models, drive trains, trim options, interior and exterior colors, and free-standing options, we calculated that the 1985 Monte Carlo had 10^9 possible build configurations.

Yes, that was 10,000,000,000, or ten billion different ways to build the car. That meant that every man, woman, and child on the planet could have a pair of brand new Monte Carlos, and no two in the world would have to be the same. It doesn't matter how many of these possible combinations they actually built. The point (and the cost) was that manufacturing had to be staffed and inventoried to be able to build every possible configuration.

It then occurred to us that we could not break this Gordian knot using some sort of incremental analysis, e.g., what is the incremental cost of adding a captain's chair option? If our hypothesis was true, we had to find a way to get into the zone of dramatic cost change to figure this out.

We settled on a simple scenario analysis. We would design and plan the optimal configuration, equipment, and staffing for five different manufacturing plants to accommodate five different build configuration scenarios: 1, 250, 2,500, 10,000, and 10^5. And we already had the answer for 10^9. We would need George Peables to provide us with twenty-five engineers, to be assigned to us full-time for two months, to design these operations from the ground up. Each of the five teams would be staffed with two industrial engineers, two mechanical engineers, and one robotic specialist. Together, they would design the manufacturing operation necessary to optimally handle each given level of complexity.

We wrote a proposal whose sole objective was to draw the cost of complexity curve for the 1985 Chevy Monte Carlo. George approved the work and assigned the engineers to us on a full-time basis.

We first decided that we wanted to isolate the true cost of the complexity itself. Replacing vinyl seats with leather seats clearly cost more money. But we were not interested in the difference in material costs—vinyl versus leather. We were only interested in the incremental manufacturing cost— the cost of multiple fixtures, the utilization impacts of differing installation times, the process impacts on previous or following assembly steps. Therefore, we took the standard cost of the Monte Carlo, with all its various options, and normalized the material cost. This meant, for our purposes, the leather in a seat cost the same as the vinyl in a seat.

Getting twenty-five engineers and technologists to understand what we were trying to do took a little time. But once they got the message, they really went at it, trying to design the optimal plant and assembly process for their given build configuration target. If you have any manufacturing background, try to imagine what the labor, equipment, and processes of a chassis assembly line might look like if every car it assembled had the same engine and transmission. Now imagine what it would take if there were four different engine options and three different transmission options. Again, whether they actually built cars with these options is beside the point. They had to be ready to build them.

While the engineers were sizing, configuring, and designing the plants, the Booz Allen team was trying to determine the component and subassembly inventory required to support each operation. How much safety stock was required to support ever more demand variability? If the plant was assembling sixty cars an hour with one build configuration, and if that design called for an AM/FM radio, then the factory would need 480 radios for every eight-hour shift. But what if each car could have either no radio, or an AM radio, or an AM/FM radio, or an AM/FM/Cassette radio? How much inventory of each would you need to handle average demand and demand variability?

When all the analysis was complete, we drew the cost of complexity curve. It was even more pronounced than the one I had drawn in George Peables' office. The surprise was how fast costs rose when complexity was introduced, and just how pervasive complexity costs truly were. The cost penalty of increasing build configurations from one to 100 was modest—about 1%. At that point, cost penalties began to escalate rapidly to about 19% at only 2,500 build configurations. The cost penalty peaked at about 22% of total costs at about 10^5 build configurations. Between that level of complexity and the Chevy Monte Carlo at 10^9 configurations, there was almost no additional cost penalty. Exhibit 16 shows the complexity cost curve.

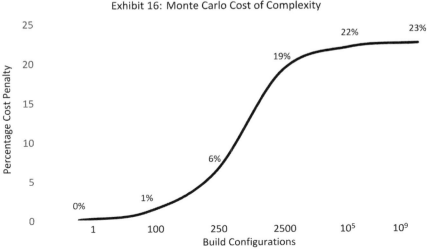

Exhibit 16: Monte Carlo Cost of Complexity

As an aside, it is interesting to remember that in 1985, Japanese cars were beginning to establish a real foothold in the North American auto market. They had a 15% price advantage over comparable domestic models, which conventional wisdom asserted was due to lower Japanese labor rates and Japanese government subsidies. However, when this complexity cost analysis was completed, Honda had 240 build configuration possibilities for their Accord. The avoidance of the complexity cost that they would have incurred had they made comparable offerings to Detroit explained 100% of their price advantage. It was spooky—almost like they had the chart!

George Peables was thrilled with the work. We went on to do another project designed to understand the impact of complexity reductions: would costs automatically come down? Or did management need to do something to make that happen? It turned out that the complexity cost curve was really the combination of two curves: one for a simple manufacturing environment in which costs escalated dramatically when complexity was introduced, the other for a complex manufacturing environment geared to handle high levels of product complexity.

Costs would automatically be reduced in the complex environment in the ordinary course of business. For example, Industrial Engineering would automatically reduce the staffing on the assembly line as significant simplifications were introduced. But once complexity decreased to a certain point, the entire manufacturing process would have to be restructured to jump to the less costly simple curve. Fundamentally new approaches to the assembly line process, only possible in the simpler environment, would need to be introduced to capture the benefits. If you are trying to imagine this, think about the kitchen in your local McDonald's versus the kitchen in a full-service restaurant.

In Exhibit 17, the complex curve shows how costs behave in a manufacturing environment staffed and equipped to handle a complex product offering. The simple curve shows the cost of a simple, repetitive manufacturing process that soars when complexity is introduced.

This was a seminal piece of analysis in the automotive industry. We began the campaign for support with a series of presentations and discussions with Ed Mertz, the General Manager of Buick. Ed was a very smart guy and a very quick study. He totally bought into the analysis, and the cost and quality benefits available to him, and he began almost immediately to engage his organization to cut options and reduce build configurations.

Exhibit 17: Two Complexity Cost Curves

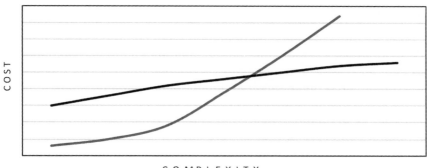

Buick was able to realize significant manufacturing cost reductions, plus they had an unintended consequence that we should have anticipated. Their quality improved, as was soon seen in customer surveys and warranty claims.

Unfortunately, George Peables and I were unable to persuade the General Managers of the other car divisions to act on these insights. Thinking about this today, I often wonder if the reason that Buick is still around, unlike Pontiac and Oldsmobile, is that they embraced this simplification initiative, and in time, realized significant reductions in their labor costs while increasing both quality and profit margins.

We tried hardest to get the Chevrolet Division to buy into these findings and their implications. But, alas, it was not to be. It took Chevy over twenty years to finally get the message. I believe this is the primary reason why Chevy sales languish behind those of Toyota and Honda today. They missed their chance to effectively compete.

Every company deals with complexity. It is a given in almost every business. But some companies and industries must deal with extraordinary complexity. The next time you are in a grocery store, stop and consider just how many unique items are offered for sale. Now try to imagine keeping track of the inventory of each, whether on a shelf or in the back room. Then try to imagine keeping track of orders and costs and prices for each item. Then try to imagine keeping track of your competitor's prices on each item. Finally, pretend that it is 1950 and try to imagine doing all of this without a computer. The retail case studies in this chapter were meant to give you a sense of this mind-numbing complexity and offer two different ways to try to deal with it.

In the GM of Canada case study, you saw another type of complexity—this one product-based, and largely self-induced. Executives throughout GM were astounded that 23% of their manufacturing costs were caused by their decision to offer consumers a broad array of choices when purchasing a car. Less is more, as Robert Browning once wrote.

Complexity costs are still pervasive today. Technology has helped enable various ways to systemically deal with complexity without incurring significant cost penalties—printing on demand in the book industry, robotics in many manufacturing industries, protocol-based documentation in the hospital industry. But complexity reduction and process simplification remain as high-potential sources of profit improvement in most companies today.

CHAPTER 12

CHALLENGE & OPTIMIZE PRICING

That which costs little is less valued.
—MIGUEL DE CERVANTES

Ron Comer, my close friend of many years, was the President of McCord Gasket Corporation in 1998. Ron was in the manufacturing plant one day and saw them making an engine gasket for a Model T Ford. When he got back to his office, he mentioned this to the head of their Aftermarket Division, John Washbish.

"How many Model T gaskets do we sell in a year?" Ron asked.

"About a thousand," John answered.

"Wow," Ron said. "And what do we charge for them?"

"$4.35 apiece," John said after looking it up.

"And what do our competitors charge?" Ron continued.

"To my knowledge, we don't have any competitors. We're the only ones who make engine gaskets for the Model T and other old cars."

"If that is true," Ron asked, "Why don't we charge a lot more? It's not like an antique car buff is going to junk his prized Model T just because the engine gasket is too expensive."

John raised the price of a Model T engine gasket to $350. And demand held constant. With the stroke of a pen, he increased their profit by $345,650 a year with no risk to demand. They applied the same logic to other antique car parts and took similar pricing actions, and generated incremental profits of over $1 million per year.

Recently, Ron told me this story and followed it by asking: "Do you know how hard you have to work to generate a $1-million-a-year sustainable cost reduction?"

It has been my experience that there is more profit left on the table due to missed pricing opportunities than any other single reason. Most are not as obvious as the McCord Gasket example. But I saw, and still see, many companies try to compete based on price, when price is not fundamental to their value proposition, nor their true basis of competition.

And often they compete after the competition is over. I can't count the number of times a retailer has said to me, after I have already declared my intention to buy something, "I can give you a 20% discount on that." I didn't ask for it. It had no impact on my purchase decision. And yet they handed over 20% of their revenue. Some will argue that the store is creating good will by doing this. I'd respond by saying that this is mighty expensive good will.

My daughter Katie used to work for a small technology service firm in Denver. I once asked the two owners, "How much of your business would you lose if you doubled your prices?"

"Half," they both responded.

"What are you waiting for?" I said, realizing that if true, they would maintain their existing revenue but only have to do half the work.

They both acted like I was crazy.

DRILL, BABY, DRILL

The cruise line industry is a decidedly fixed-cost operation. The ship, the fuel, and the officers and crew expenses are the same regardless of how many passengers take any particular cruise. About the only variable expense is the cost of the groceries. And midnight buffets notwithstanding, food costs are surprisingly low. When a cruise line sells over 92 percent of its available capacity, they print money. But if less than 80 percent of the cabins are occupied, they lose their keister.

In the mid-1980s, there was a relatively mild recession in the United States. Lots of folks cut back on their discretionary spending, and no surprise, that included Caribbean cruise vacations. As demand for cruises fell, one competitor, Carnival Cruise Line, decided to take decisive action. In an effort to fill up their ships, they announced that they would offer free airfare from anywhere in the continental United States to anyone booking a cruise on Carnival. Of course, all of Carnival's competitors had no choice but to quickly follow suit.

Many people thought Carnival was nuts, because once their competitors followed their lead, they would gain no relative advantage. They would simply give away a lot of money. I always thought that Carnival was dumb like a fox. They were in a much stronger marketing and financial position than their competitors to absorb the new expense. And I'm sure they saw the boom in the demand for cruises that free airfare would create once the recession was over. Whether they were prescient or just lucky, their strategy worked. Carnival added eight cruise ships to its five-ship fleet from 1992 through 1999, and emerged as the unchallenged industry leader.

The announcement of free airfare caused havoc for most competitors. One such company was Norwegian Cruise Line, or as it was known in 1983, Norwegian Caribbean Cruise Line. NCCL's CEO, Ron Zeller, requested proposals from several management consulting firms to help the company deal with the issue. I led the team from Booz Allen, and we were fortunate that Ron selected us to do the work. The issue was clear. Prior to free airfare, NCCL had annual revenues of about $250 million and made about $35 million in profit. Free airfare cost them $65 million per year. Overnight, this expense went from nonexistent to the largest single line item in their budget. And NCCL went from making $35 million a year to losing $30 million a year—all in an instant.

To deal with this situation, we had to address several potential areas of profit improvement. Several staff members concentrated on cost reduction, both ship-side and shore-side. Other staff looked at marketing and sales, and tried to identify opportunities to increase demand. A third group focused on pricing. The pricing work is the subject of this case study.

We began with a theoretical understanding of pricing. Price elasticity is a measure used in economics to show how the demand for a good or service responds to a change in price. More precisely, it gives the percentage change in quantity demanded in response to a one percent change in price. For example, wine has historically had a price elasticity of -1.0, which means that a price increase of 10% for your favorite chardonnay will likely result in a 10% reduction in demand. We needed to understand price elasticity in the cruise industry in order to assess NCCL's pricing.

At that time, NCCL had six ships and offered a variety of three-, four-, and seven-day cruises throughout the Caribbean. Their principal competitors—Carnival, Royal Caribbean, and Holland America—had a similar number of ships and offered similar cruise packages and itineraries. And each cruise ship offered a number of different types of accommodations—outside cabins, inside cabins, standard cabins, deluxe cabins, suites.

Prices varied by ship, cruise date, duration, itinerary, and cabin type. But even so, most prices fell between $1,200 and $1,500 per passenger for a one-week cruise in an average cabin. NCCL consistently appeared at the low end of this range. We decided to randomly pick twelve different cruise dates and to constrain the analysis to one-week Western Caribbean cruises departing from Miami. Further, since every ship offered them, we decided to use the prices for outside deluxe cabins as the basis of comparison.

We searched cruise line brochures and other industry data to determine these prices for NCCL and each of their three main competitors. These four companies had collectively operated twenty ships exclusively in the Caribbean during the past year. That meant that with twelve sample cruises for each ship, we had two hundred and forty pricing data points.

Given the highly-regulated nature of the maritime industry, we also had historical passenger manifest data for each ship and cruise for the past year. We could calculate demand and occupancy for each cruise in our pricing database.

Thus, we were able to plot a set of two hundred-plus data points of cruise occupancy, as a surrogate for relative demand, and price for NCCL and their three largest competitors for a week-long cruise in a deluxe outside cabin. When we first saw the results, we were certain that we had made a mistake. Demand appeared to be completely uncorrelated with price. This defied both common sense and all known laws of economics. Price

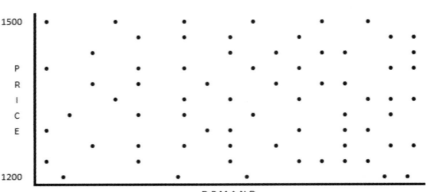

Exhibit 18: One Week Caribbean Cruise Price Elasticity

went down. Demand went down. Or demand went up. Or demand stayed the same. For the first time in history, there was total price inelasticity for a product. The company could price the cruise at any amount they chose within the range from $1200 to $1500, and demand would stay constant, as shown in Exhibit 18.

We checked and rechecked the data; all to no avail. I remember sitting in a conference room one evening at about 7:30 when one of my colleagues said, "Maybe we're too focused in on a narrow range of options. Why don't we look at pricing and demand for an array of vacation options, and see if that sheds any light?"

We researched and analyzed average prices and annual demand for a wide range of possibilities and normalized their costs to a one-week trip: African safaris, four-star resort hotels, chartered jet excursions, driving national park visits, local camping trips, Caribbean cruises, and more. Then we plotted these prices and demands, shown in Exhibit 19. Eureka! Rationality was back. The higher the relative price, the lower the relative demand. But how were we to explain the anomaly of Caribbean cruise pricing and demand?

Exhibit 19: One Week Vacation Price Elasticity

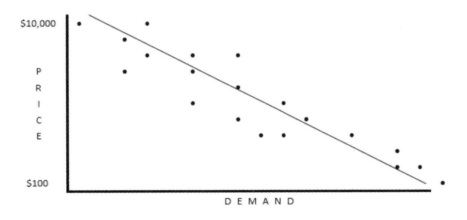

Someone observed that the weekly per person vacation prices ranged from $10,000 to $100. Maybe our weekly cruise prices represented more of a point than a range of options. Folks decide what sort of a vacation they want to take and the approximate price they are willing to pay, and then they start looking at the options available to them. Once they get to that point, price is no longer the determining factor. Doesn't it make sense that once a couple decides to spend the money on a one-week cruise in the Caribbean, they are probably indifferent whether the price per person is $1,200 or $1,400?

We explored this hypothesis and did some more analysis. The more we understood, the more sense it made. And if it was true, NCCL could raise their prices to the top of the competitive range with very little risk of losing demand. Given their situation, Ron Zeller thought they had very little to lose. So, when the next brochure was issued two months later, he increased their prices accordingly, as shown graphically in Exhibit 20. The small point that is boxed on the graph represents the cruise price analysis which ranged from $1,200 to $1,500 per week. The box below the graph is a magnification of that point and shows how NCCL raised their prices to the top of the competitive range.

Exhibit 20: One Week Vacation Price Elasticity

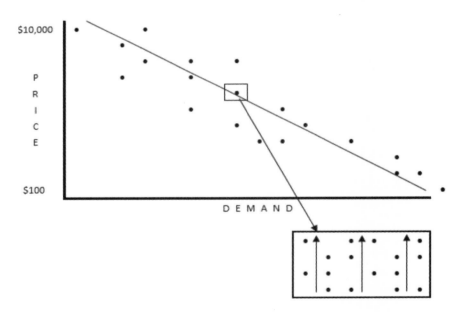

Three months later, NCCL realized prices were up by 11%, and revenue was up by 15%. It is true that demand was increasing because the recession was easing, but the primary driver of the increase was the higher prices. This action alone solved almost half of the financial problem posed by free airfare. If demand is unaffected, price increases equal free money.

When the answer keeps eluding you, keep drilling down in the analysis. Drill, baby, drill!

OUR MOTHER OF MERCY IS NOT A THREAT

My partner John Smith and I co-authored an article about strategic planning in academic medical centers (AMCs). It was published in *Academic Medicine*, the journal of the Association of American Medical Colleges in July 1997. In the article, we wrote: "One of the poorer assumptions made by AMCs today is that the market for health care services is economically rational, which implies that price is a primary determinant of demand. This assumption seems to be accepted as an article of faith, undisturbed by the evidence all around that it is not the case. At a minimum, one would expect AMCs, with their inherent price disadvantage, to maintain and extend, if not exploit, whatever irrationality exists in the market for as long as possible."[16]

This criticism was most typified in some strategy formulation work that we did for Johns Hopkins Hospital in Baltimore. Our client was the President of the hospital and health system, Dr. James Block.

As part of our work, we delved into their operating costs per procedure and compared them to those of their competitors. Hospitals were then required to submit detailed records of their volumes and costs to Medicare. The Medicare Cost Reports provided a rich trove of operating data about virtually all hospitals in the country.

We were doing this work in 1993. Medicare reimbursed hospitals based on a standard price for each designated procedure performed by the hospital. These were called Diagnostic-Related Groups. Likewise, in 1993, insurance companies reimbursed hospitals based on a negotiated fee for each procedure. These varied from hospital to hospital. The point of this was that we could use Medicare Cost Reports for various procedures to capture costs, and insurance company reimbursement rates to capture price for selected procedures for Hopkins and their various competitors.

---

[16] Kurt Krauss and John Smith, "Rejecting Conventional Wisdom: How Academic Medical Centers Can Regain Their Leadership Positions," *Academic Medicine*, 72, no. 7 (July 1997): 572.

Johns Hopkins' costs were predictably higher than those of local, non-teaching hospitals in the Baltimore area. But they were comparable to their industry peers: Columbia-Presbyterian Hospital, the Cleveland Clinic, and the Mayo Clinic.

Because their competition was local, and they knew that their local competitors had lower costs on virtually every procedure performed, Johns Hopkins Hospital was in perpetual cost reduction mode. They accepted as an article of faith that demand was driven, in large part, by price, and that price was, of necessity, determined by cost. Initiative after initiative was launched to, for example, change the mix of RNs to aides from 50%/50% to 30%/70%, to increase RN staffing metrics from four patients per RN to five patients per RN, to standardize on one type of surgical suture, and force all surgeons to use it. Given the complex nature of hospital operations and the relatively high acuity (intensity of care required) of Hopkins' patients, rarely was any sustainable cost reduction achieved.

Not surprisingly, the reimbursement rates provided by private insurance companies also varied from hospital to hospital. It depended upon who was the better negotiator and upon other less tangible factors, including patient and doctor preference and clinical reputation, as we will see.

We selected one procedure—heart bypass surgery—to bore in on, and understand cost, price, and demand in detail, and their likely impact on the hospital's market and strategic position. We also used Medicare Cost Report data to create comparative statistics for their largest cardiac services competitor in Baltimore, Mercy Hospital.

The analysis showed that Hopkins' propensity to assume that normal price elasticity applied to the market for cardiac surgery was a dangerous and misleading assumption. Exhibit 21 shows what we found.

This analysis clearly showed that price was not the primary determinant of demand for cardiac services in Baltimore. In fact, it appeared to have no effect. As Hopkins' costs and prices rose over time, so did demand. And as Mercy Hospital's costs and prices declined over time, so did demand. Something else besides price was clearly driving demand.

We did market research and held a few focus groups to confirm our hypotheses about this market dynamic. Not surprisingly, we found that reputation was the primary factor driving a patient's choice of a hospital when facing heart surgery. This also explained why insurance companies agreed to include Hopkins in their coverage plans even though their costs

Exhibit 21: Price Inelasticity of Cardiac Surgery Procedures

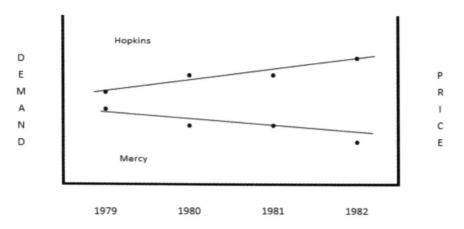

were 15% to 20% higher than those of other local hospitals. It would have been a non-starter for corporate customers if Johns Hopkins was excluded from their policies.

✳

Pricing may be the most misunderstood subject in American business. Many companies wrongly assume that price is the primary determinant of the demand for their products or services. This is rarely the case. Functionality, quality, service, or availability is usually the main driver of demand. Or as a colleague of mine once said: "Price simply breaks ties." That was the case with Johns Hopkins Hospital. Their capability, quality, and service were hardly tied with those of Mercy Hospital. And yet Hopkins management behaved as if they were.

The NCCL case study showed that, often times, industry pricing is very nuanced. In this case, it was being able to see that price ranges were more important than price points.

For some companies, like Amazon, price is a key element of their value proposition. For other companies, like cruise lines and hospitals, it is not. Don't try to compete on price unless you have decided that price will be your basis of competition. There is often a significant opportunity for a company to increase their profitability simply by raising their prices. And those who have multiple stores, locations, or coverage areas can easily experiment with their pricing with very little risk. I could easily test the price elasticity of this book by pricing it at one amount in some bookstores and at a higher amount in other bookstores, and then comparing the sales results of each group. In my experience, few such companies take advantage of their opportunity to test pricing in this way.

This second section, *The Change Agent's Tool Kit*, has defined what I consider to be the six primary opportunities for improving a company's performance, and offered real case studies about each: changing the value proposition, aligning the organization with it, streamlining processes, improving utilization, reducing product or process complexity, and optimizing prices.

The next section presents a detailed case study of a truly transformative change initiative that required massive restructuring built around almost all the opportunities just presented.

THE CHANGE AGENT'S DESTINY

THE PATIENT-FOCUSED HOSPITAL:
A CASE STUDY IN TRANSFORMATIONAL CHANGE

Everyone can rise above their circumstances and achieve success if they
are dedicated to and passionate about what they do.
—NELSON MANDELA

I n the mid-1980s, many U.S. hospitals were in a state of panic. In the past, insurance companies like Blue Cross Blue Shield and programs like Medicare had been willing to reimburse hospitals based on their actual patient care costs. But that was changing rapidly. Insurance companies were beginning to negotiate fixed prices and discounts for various procedures with individual hospitals and hospital chains, and they controlled considerable patient volume, meaning they had great leverage: "Agree to this price or your patients will be sent to the hospital down the street."

At the same time, Medicare was changing their reimbursement scheme to pay a set price for each procedure performed or condition treated. They created something called Diagnostic-Related Groups (DRGs) and established a fixed payment amount for each one. For example, a hip replacement operation with no complications might have had a reimbursement rate of $36,550. Whether the patient was in the hospital for four days or seven, the reimbursement stayed the same. The price was set at what Medicare calculated that a reasonably efficient hospital using accepted protocols of care could achieve, plus a reasonable mark-up, adjusted for geographic location and other exogenous factors. This caused major problems for perhaps 50% of the hospitals in the country, and it ushered in a new era of intense cost pressure in the industry.

By the mid-eighties, I was well along in building a Global Service Operations practice within Booz Allen. I had done significant work for retailers, banks, insurance companies, and cruise lines. I had also teamed up with my partners in the Healthcare practice to do some operations work in hospitals, but most of it had been basic cost reduction work; nothing much to write home about.

I had numerous conversations with John Smith, Booz Allen's Global Healthcare Practice Leader, about working together on something major and strategic for a large U.S. hospital. One day he mentioned Lakeland Regional Medical Center in Lakeland, Florida as a good candidate for such an assignment. They were a large, well-run hospital with a smart, progressive CEO named Jack Stephens. John and Jack had a personal and professional relationship that went back ten years. I encouraged John to try to arrange a meeting for the three of us. He did and we met.

In 1986, Lakeland Regional Medical Center (LRMC) was an acute care hospital with 650 beds and a regional trauma center. It had a sterling reputation for quality, and was the number two hospital in the State of Florida in cost per case and other measures of cost-effectiveness.

LRMC was adapting to the new reimbursement schemes better than most of its peers. This was not a hospital that was struggling or under siege. They were financially, clinically, and operationally sound. In my view, the best time to rethink your overall operating strategy is when you are in a strong position, both internally and competitively. Otherwise, your efforts will undoubtedly be compromised by immediate issues and the need for short-term improvements.

Thankfully, Jack Stephens understood this, and when John Smith called, he agreed to meet with us. We met with him in his office in Lakeland. We had a long conversation about the hospital and its performance, both absolute and relative. That's where I learned of his statewide ranking and his very favorable cost, quality, and patient satisfaction performance. Jack came across as confident and knowledgeable, but not overly comfortable or satisfied. He knew that the entire industry was undergoing massive change and he wanted to be sure that he and his hospital stayed ahead of the curve.

The discussion turned to operations strategy and my relevant experience. I admitted up front that while I had worked in a few hospitals, I really didn't have any great insights into ways to dramatically restructure their operations or what might be achieved as a result. I told him that I appreciated the extraordinary complexity of hospital operations, and the reality that lives were always at stake.

Then I began to describe some the operations strategy work that I had been a part of over recent years. I explained in some detail the cost-of-complexity work that I had led at General Motors of Canada. I described the approach to the analysis and the insights that it had produced. I shared our conclusions about the pervasive cost of complexity and the opportunity to reduce it. I used a flip chart to draw the automotive cost of complexity curve and to provide other details about our findings.

I continued by describing a seminal piece of strategy work that I had been part of at Deere & Company six years earlier. Again, I shared facts and analysis and conclusions about the work and its strategic impact on Deere's operations. I also shared the specifics of the major supply chain management assignment that we had completed for Target Stores that allowed them to save millions of dollars each year in store labor and inventory carrying costs.

At some point, I said to Jack: "I don't know exactly how we would approach a hospital operations strategy assignment. But it is analyses and insights like these that will point the way. It's the only way to discover a higher quality, more cost-effective, more sustainable operating paradigm for the hospital."

"Okay," Jack said, "write me a proposal."

–PHASE I–

We wrote Jack a proposal to perform an extensive diagnostic review of all the operations at Lakeland Regional. It described in detail the data that we would collect and the various work steps that we would complete. It explained some of the analyses that might provide actionable insight in the end. But again, neither we nor anyone else had ever undertaken such a strategic look at hospital operations, so it was impossible to propose exactly what we would do. Much of this work would require us to follow our experience and instincts wherever they led us.

We said that the work would be led by yours truly and would be staffed by a full-time team of three or four experienced operations professionals, none of whom would have had any hospital experience. John Smith and another partner from Booz Allen's Healthcare practice, Phil Lathrop, would serve as Consulting Officers and would bring an industry perspective to the team when and where appropriate. We said that this work would take four months to complete and that our professional fees would be $500,000.

In 1986, this was an extraordinary amount of money for a hospital to pay for outside consulting assistance, particularly when the outcome was so unknown. Was this a smart investment or a dumb investment? Nobody really knew. My colleagues and I had great confidence in the potential for this work. And that must have resonated with Jack Stephens. "Go big or go home!" must have been Jack's motto. He approved the project and off we went.

I staffed the core team with three colleagues from the Operations practice: Gary Shows, a Principal; Adam Zauder, a Senior Associate; and Bill Leander, an Associate. Other professionals rotated on and off the project as needed. Of course, my partners John Smith and Phil Lathrop interacted with the team and the client on a regular basis.

The balance of this section describes the operations strategy work—from diagnostic analysis through implementation—that we did at Lakeland Regional Medical Center from 1986 through 1992. I have presented numerous charts and graphs to describe the existing and new operating paradigm of the hospital. Some of the numbers I can still recall with precision. I had to create others based on my memories of the work, but they are very representative of what we actually found.

I was helped in this process by referring to a book that was written by Phil Lathrop, the Consulting Officer on all the work that we did at LRMC. Phil's book is *Restructuring Health Care: The Patient-Focused Paradigm.* It was published in 1993 by Jossey-Bass, Inc. While I did not directly quote from his book, nor did I copy any of his charts or analysis, his work did refresh my memory substantially.

CHAPTER 13

KEY DIAGNOSTIC ANALYSES

Analysis is the art of creation through destruction.
—P.S. BABER

The team was given an office at LRMC and we started to work. We collected massive amounts of data on cost and utilization and quality, we mapped key operating processes, reviewed job descriptions, interviewed hundreds of people, and completed extensive work sampling. We also reviewed policies; observed surgeries; analyzed demand and demand patterns; and reviewed the inputs, processing logic, and outputs of all financial, clinical, and operating information systems. Finally, we built the current value-added structure of the hospital. The results were startling.

OPERATING COSTS

For all the blinking lights, impressive technology, and shiny new equipment, hospitals are still labor-intensive businesses. In fact, the only industries that I can think of that are more labor-intensive are agriculture, construction, hospitality, food service, and professional services. According to Wikipedia, four of the seven largest non-governmental employers in Central Ohio are hospitals or hospital systems. In 2016, they employed almost 50,000 people.

When we began work at LRMC, one of our first tasks was to immerse ourselves in their income statement. We made sure we understood the definitions of all the line items in both the cost and revenue categories.

Pricing in hospitals at that time bore little resemblance to reality. LRMC had standard prices for every procedure they performed and every condition they treated. But these were the prices that private patients with no insurance were asked to pay, and private patients comprised less than 5% of the hospital's demand. The other 95%[+] of demand was reimbursed through Medicare, Medicaid, or private insurance, which all paid a negotiated amount that had nothing to do with the hospital's "standard" prices. Thus, the operant revenue figure was Net Revenue. The 1985 income statement showed net to revenues of $218 million, as shown in Exhibit 22.

Exhibit 22: LRMC 1985 Income Statement

Gross Revenue			$462,000
	Discounts		-149,000
	Write-Offs		-95,000
Net Revenue			$218,000
Expenses			
	Labor		
		Wages & Salaries	97,200
		Employee Benefits	17,200
	Supplies		
		Med/Surg Supplies	30,200
		Pharmaceuticals & Blood	10,400
	Facilities		
		Utilities	2,800
		Maintenance	5,000
	Insurance		2,200
	Outside Services		
		Contractors	8,200
		Professional Fees	6,400
	Depreciation & Amortization		9,600
	Interest		6,000
	Other		4,800
Total Expenses			$200,000
Contribution to Reserves			$18,000

Expense categories were more straightforward. After researching each one, we found they were generally what they appeared to be. Since LRMC was a tax-exempt, not-for-profit institution, they were prohibited from making a profit. Instead, any surplus funds were placed into reserve accounts to fund future capital needs or operating losses. That said, Lakeland's operating margin of 8.3% was very strong for a hospital in 1986.

We looked at several years of cost data and questioned any trend, upward or downward. We then combined some cost categories and assembled the basic cost structure of the hospital:

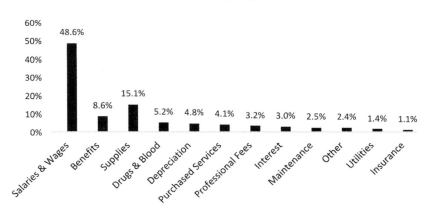

Exhibit 23: LRMC Cost Structure

Look at the first two cost categories in Exhibit 23—salaries, wages, and benefits. They totaled 57.2% of total costs. This is what a labor-intensive operation looks like. Supply costs ran to 15%, or if you include drugs and blood, to 20%. But all other categories were each less than 5% of total cost. Where would you guess that the improvement leverage resided?

CAPITAL COSTS

Looking at this same exhibit, you can see the capital-intensity of the business. Capital costs are captured by depreciation and amortization. For you non-accounting types, here is how it works: When a hospital purchases a capital asset, say an X-ray machine for $75,000, it would be misleading to record this as an annual expense, because the hospital will get use and value out of it for many years to come.

Suppose that the estimated useful life of the X-ray machine is ten years. Then, an accountant would add $75,000 to the balance sheet, and would relieve the balance sheet and charge the income statement for $7,500 each year for ten years. This is known as depreciation. If the asset was intangible, like a technology license or a patent, it would be called amortization.

Thus, the annual capital cost of the business is represented by total annual depreciation and amortization, in this case 4.8%. Labor costs at LRMC were 11.9 times greater than capital costs. In a capital-intensive industry, like petroleum refining, for example, capital costs are usually more than labor costs.

Looked at another way, Jack Stephens, Lakeland's CEO, could double his capital assets—double the number of beds from 650 to 1,300, double CAT scan machines from two to four, double operating rooms from twelve to twenty-four, double everything—if he could reduce labor costs by only 8.4%. This realization will become very important later.

ORGANIZATIONAL STRUCTURE

Lakeland was organized like most hospitals of the day: by function. Jack Stephens had ten direct reports. Each led a stand-alone functional department, like Nursing or IT. As outlined in Exhibit 24, you might be surprised that there are no doctors shown in the organization chart. In the 1980s, it was rare for hospitals to employ doctors except for radiologists or pathologists. The doctors were independent and were linked to the hospital

Exhibit 24: LRMC Organization Chart

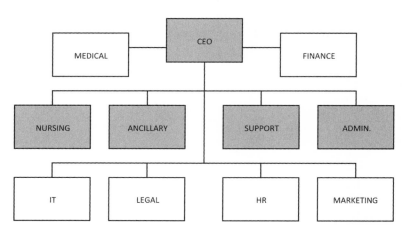

through the Medical Director, who granted admitting privileges to qualified local doctors.

The areas shaded in gray were the key line departments. Ninety-five
percent of all employees worked in one of these four departments.

Exhibit 25: LRMC Line Organizations

NURSING	ANCILLIARY SVCS
Floor Nursing	Radiology
ER Nursing	Pathology Lab
OR Nursing	Operating Rooms
ICU Nursing	Emergency Room
SUPPORT SVCS	ADMINISTRATIVE SVCS
Food Service	Admitting
Housekeeping	Patient Records
Transport	Billing
Engineering	Clerical

Each line department tended to be a multi-level hierarchy of delegat-
ed functional responsibility. Here are how the key operating departments
were structured:

Exhibit 26: LRMC Typical Functional Hierarchy

It is perhaps more interesting to diagram the organization from the viewpoint of a staff member looking up at the hierarchy. In this case, we'll look at a typical staff registered nurse (RN):

Exhibit 27: LRMC Bottom-Up Org Chart

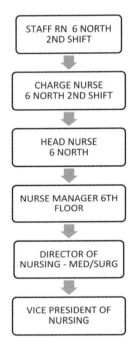

Note the hierarchical structure and narrow functional scope of the Nursing department. Yes, the staff nurse saw to most of the bedside clinical care provided to patients. But he/she was not responsible or accountable for many other aspects of patient care and patient support: drawing blood, respiratory therapy treatments, housekeeping, transport, and other centralized services.

FACILITIES

The physical layout of the hospital was based around patient care units and centralized services. LRMC was an eight-story building shaped like a giant H. Each floor had four wings, two on each end, with a wide connector in the center that housed storage, offices, and common areas. There were twenty-six inpatient care units—four units on each of six floors and two on another floor—all housed in the wings. Each unit had from ten to thirty beds. They were designated for various patient types: critical care, psychiatric, general medical/surgical, cardiac, orthopedics, ICU, and so on. The admitting staff attempted to put patients on the unit and floor designated for the kind of care they needed, but during periods of high occupancy, this was often not possible.

The first two floors and the basement housed central ancillary and support services—admitting, radiology, lab, food service and the cafeteria, operating rooms, and the emergency room. It probably looked a lot like the hospitals with which you are familiar today.

Because of this facility design, and the location of the centralized ancillary services, transportation of patients and staff was a major issue at LRMC. Later in this section, we'll see just how many resources were used to move staff and patients around the hospital.

JOBS

When most people think about the range of jobs in a hospital, they think of doctors, nurses, aides, admitting clerks, X-ray techs, and the like. But it is not that simple. For many years, most positions in a hospital had become ever more specialized. It used to be that your nurse would draw blood for lab tests and perform simple respiratory therapies. By 1986, we had phlebotomists who did nothing but draw blood and dedicated therapists who spent all day administering simple respiratory treatments. Further, to get the maximum utilization from more expensive RN staff, hospitals divided their work into tasks and brought in lower-paid licensed practical nurses (LPNs) and aides to offload this lower-value work.

We began our investigation by looking at the number of employees in various job categories.

One of the most telling numbers in Exhibit 28 is the number of clerical support staff—648. Remember that LRMC had 650 beds in 1986. This means that conceptually we could have assigned one clerk to each inpatient. The clerk could then have followed the patient around and handled all documentation, and we could have eliminated all the systems and processes that were required to keep track of patient activity and billing information.

Exhibit 28: LRMC Employees by Category

Managers & Supervisors	255
Administrative Professionals	135
Clerical Support	648
Nurses & Technicians	2336
Laborers	850
Total	4224

Then we looked at the training and educational requirements for all non-management employees in the hospital. For all the perceptions about the high-tech nature of heath care, fully 50% of the jobs at LRMC required a high school diploma or less. As shown in Exhibit 29, these included clerical staff, food service workers, transport aides, housekeepers, and even some technicians and clinical staff.

Exhibit 29: LRMC Staff Educational Requirements

Graduate Degree	59
Bachelor's Degree	188
Registered Nurses	941
Associate Degree	425
Trade or Technical Training	358
High School Diploma or Less	1998
Total	3969

Finally, we looked at each unique job classification that existed at LRMC and cataloged how many full-time employees (FTEs) held each position. Exhibit 30 shows that the hospital had 565 unique positions, 39% of which had only one full-time employee. We didn't yet understand quite what this meant, but we knew that it was somehow significant.

Exhibit 30: FTEs per Job Classification

Paid FTEs	Positions
1	220
2-5	118
6-10	45
11-25	38
26-50	17
50+	9
	565

WORK FLOWS/PROCESSES

The team spent considerable time documenting key processes and work flows in the hospital: ordering and completing a lab test, ordering and dispensing pharmaceuticals, moving patients to and from the operating room, and providing and documenting bedside nursing care, for example.

In Chapter 5, we saw the process for ordering and completing an Xray for an inpatient. As was described, this process involved twenty-two different steps if the patient was in their room when the transport aide first arrived. If not, five steps were repeated multiple times until the patient could be found. Taking the actual X-ray was simply one step. Nine different hospital employees were required to perform this relatively simple process. Two different computer systems were used. And the patient had to wait upwards of forty-five minutes at various points during the process.

Contrast this with your family physician's office: your doctor decides she wants a chest X-ray. Her RN walks you down the hall into the X-ray room and takes the X-ray. You go back to the exam room while the RN develops the film and puts it onto the screen for the doctor to read. She's back in the exam room in ten minutes and says: "Everything looks good."

That is not meant to say that a board certified radiologist shouldn't be involved in this process; only that the process itself need not be so lengthy and complicated.

Exhibit 31 shows the X-ray flow chart from Chapter 5 in a somewhat different format. Notice how much time is spent documenting and dispatching, and how long the patient has to wait. These activities do not add

Exhibit 31: LRMC X-Ray Flow Chart

MD Orders X-Ray	→	RN Delivers Order to Clerk	→	Clerk Enters Order into System
Radiology Logs Order	→	Radiology Contacts Transport	→	Transport Dispatches Transporter
Transporter Travels to Patient Room	→	Patient in Room?	→	If Not, Contact Dispatcher and Start Over
If Yes, Move Patient to Radiology	→	Patient Waits in Lobby	→	Patient Moved to Treatment Room
X-Ray Taken	→	Patient Moved to Lobby	→	Patient Waits in Lobby
Radiology Contacts Transport	→	Transport Logs Request	→	Transport Dispatches Transporter
Transporter Travels to Radiology	→	Transporter Moves Patient to Their Room	→	Transporter Notifies Unit Clerk

value to patients, and in fact become major irritants.

On the next four pages, you'll see the process flow chart in 1986 for getting a patient from their room, to the operating room for a gall bladder removal, into the recovery area, and back to their room. Due to space considerations, I have not described the work step in each box. Instead, I've simply shown the first word of the work step. Had I included the entire description, this flow chart would have continued for another six pages.

Exhibit 32: LRMC Surgery Process Flow Chart

Pre-Op Lab Test

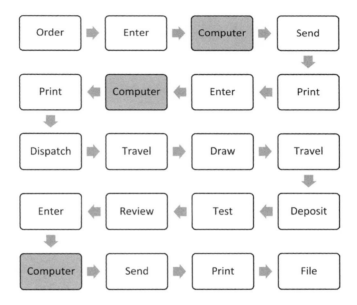

Pre-Op Sedation

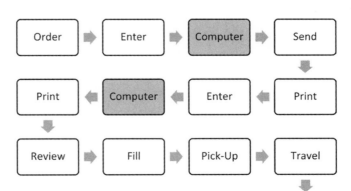

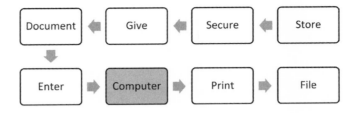

Nursing Unit Prep

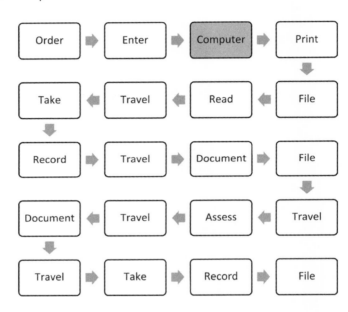

Transport to Operating Room

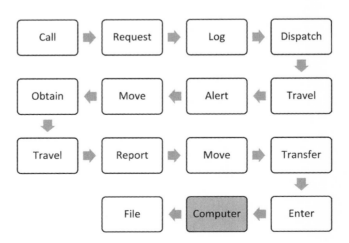

Pre-Op

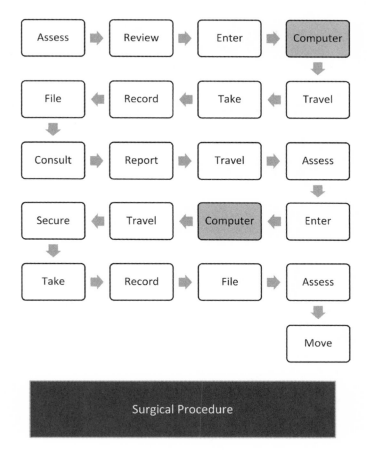

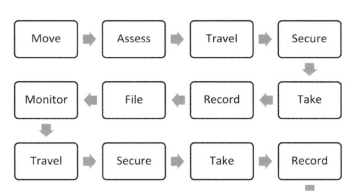

Post-Op Recovery

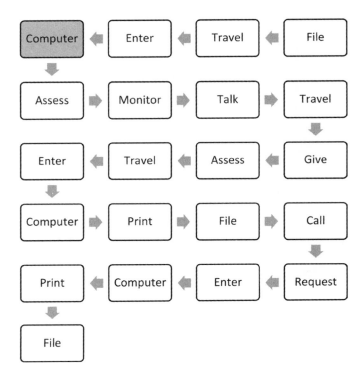

Transport to Room

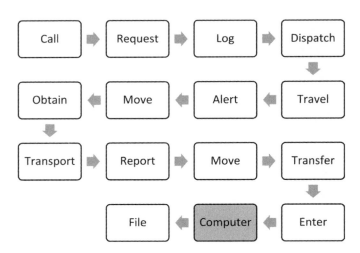

Four pages of little boxes and one hundred and forty process steps. And the entire two-hour surgery involving surgeons, scrub nurses, documenting nurses, anesthesiologists, and other techs and aides only counted as one process step.

Each work step would have said something like "Enter pharmacy order into pharmacy system," or "Transport patient to the operating room," or "Record vital signs on the patient record."

In all, it took thirty-four different employees to complete these tasks, not counting anyone working in the operating room. Collectively, they were part of eight departments, ultimately reporting to four vice presidents. The patient was present for sixty-nine (48%) of the process steps, and directly interacted with twenty-two of these employees.

Computers were accessed and information was entered on twelve separate occasions. This required the use of four different systems, none of which was linked to the other three. Each contained a stand-alone database.

The type of employee required to complete each step in the process was revealing. Fifty-seven percent of the work was performed by clerks and aides.

Exhibit 33: LRMC Employees by Category

MD	7
Tech	23
RN	34
Aide	38
Clerk	42
	144

Finally, we found that not one employee of the hospital could map this process from end to end. Most people knew several of the steps before theirs and maybe a couple of steps after. The length and complexity of this process seemed to clearly result from the functional organizational structure, narrowly defined jobs, and a heavy reliance on centralized services.

CONTINUITY OF CARE

If you've ever been a patient in a hospital or have been treated in an emergency room, I would hazard to guess that you interacted with an amazing assortment of people—doctors, nurses, aides, techs, other techs, clerks. This is not ideal from a patient care perspective.

Patients with serious medical issues are usually not comfortable with a constant stream of new people coming into and out of their rooms. Many of these staff members ask questions that have already been asked of and answered by the patient several times. That is not reassuring to them.

We called this seemingly endless stream of employees "faces in the parade," and we documented that number for a variety of procedures and stays at the hospital. Here is a typical parade for a four-day surgical procedure.

Exhibit 34: Faces in the Parade

Category	Number of Contacts
Nursing	32
Dietary	12
Ancillary Services	8
Central Transport	6
Housekeeping	5
Other	4
	67

DEMAND PATTERNS

Demand for hospital procedures, both inpatient and outpatient, was reasonably stable for the hospital as a whole, but was highly variable by patient unit. We captured the bed capacity, occupancy, and the standard deviation of demand for each unit, and the hospital in total. In a normal distribution, demand will fall within +/- one standard deviation 68% of the time, and two standard deviations 95% of the time.

The hospital's 650 bed capacity was divided among twenty-six different units. Most were general medical/surgical floors where the widest range of patients were provided care. Admissions tried to place similar patients on the same unit, but they often came up short.

Exhibit 35: 1985 LRMC Inpatient Demand

Unit	Description	Bed Capacity	Average Occupancy	Peak Census	Lowest Census	Standard Deviation
2E	ICU/CICU	20	90%	20	10	5.3
2S	Neonatal	10	80%	10	6	4.6
3E	Med/Surg	25	90%	25	10	8.3
3S	Med/Surg	25	83%	25	9	6.3
3W	Med/Surg	25	82%	25	12	8.5
3N	Med/Surg	25	91%	25	10	7.9
4E	Ortho	30	95%	30	11	8.8
4S	Neuro	30	90%	30	9	6.4
4W	Med/Surg	30	81%	30	6	8.4
4N	Med/Surg	30	83%	30	11	7.3
5E	Cardiac	25	79%	25	8	6.6
5S	Cardiology	25	82%	25	6	7.9
5W	Oncology	25	89%	25	7	8.5
5N	Oncology	25	84%	25	12	8.5
6E	Med/Surg	25	88%	25	8	6.3
6S	Med/Surg	25	82%	25	9	5.1
6W	Med/Surg	25	79%	25	6	6.3
6N	Pediatrics	25	74%	25	14	6.5
7E	Maternity	30	75%	30	12	6.1
7S	Ob/Gyn	30	75%	30	9	8.4
7W	Med/Surg	30	88%	30	8	5.5
7N	Med/Surg	30	89%	30	7	9.1
8E	Med/Surg	20	91%	20	9	7.4
8S	Med/Surg	20	90%	20	7	8.3
8W	Med/Surg	20	85%	20	8	8.2
8B	Med/Surg	20	84%	20	6	9.2
Sum of Units		650	85%	650	230	189.7
Hospital Total		650	85%	650	480	83.2

Note the extreme demand variability at the unit level. Take 6W: it has a bed capacity of twenty-five and ran at 79% occupancy during 1985. That was lower than the hospital average of 85%. The standard deviation of their daily demand was 6.3. That meant that their daily census consistently ranged from twelve to twenty-five.

The standard deviation of demand at the unit level was 34% of the average daily census. At the hospital level, the standard deviation drops to 15% of the average daily census, a 227% reduction in variability. This, too, will be important later.

SYSTEMS

The computer age began in the late 1950s, but it was not until the early 1970s that hardware and software were routinely being deployed in American businesses. When I began working at a progressive manufacturing company in 1971, all records were manual: inventory records, purchase orders, part specifications, factory orders, you name it. It was not until 1972 that we began to introduce formal, computerized purchasing, production, and inventory management systems.

Information technology (IT) in hospitals evolved on the same timeline. In 1986, there were seven IT systems operating at LRMC, but each one of them was unintegrated and stand-alone, and supported only one functional area. They included:

- An admissions system
- A pharmacy system
- A laboratory system
- A radiology system
- An accounting system
- A billing system
- A medical coding system

All documentation of patient care on the nursing units or in the operating room was manual. Nurses wrote nursing notes in longhand to document all the care that they delivered. Unit clerks assembled patient files consisting of written doctors' orders, written nurses' notes, lab results, radiology reports, pharmaceutical records, and every other aspect of a patient's care. A four-day length of stay for a gall bladder removal patient would typically result in a file that was five inches thick. That would be sent to medical records for transposition into the medical coding system, which in turn would be sent to the Billing Department for entry into the billing system.

While this seems like a cumbersome and inefficient environment, it was typical of the time. That said, it was an area that demanded attention and would become an enabler of many of the structural changes that were anticipated.

VALUE-ADDED STRUCTURE

Every enterprise takes a collection of purchased inputs—raw materials and component parts, assets, and services—and converts them into a product or service available for sale. What the enterprise does to accomplish this is known as their value-added. Said another way, it is all the various activities that are performed by all categories of labor to create the product or service from purchased materials and capital assets. The final major diagnostic analysis that we completed was the construction of the value-added structure of Lakeland Regional.

At LRMC, we captured about 350,000 point-in-time observations of all classifications of staff across all departments, all days of the week, and all hours of the day. Every day, each one of four Booz Allen staff members would develop a one-minute walking route around the facilities on a specific floor, and would select ten different employees working in various areas of that floor for observation. Then, as they walked the route each minute, they would put a tick mark next to the activity the given employee was engaged in when the Booz Allen staff member first saw them. The activities that we specified were:

- Medical, Technical, or Clinical Work
- Clinical Documentation
- Food Service or Hotel Work
- Travel—With Patient
- Institutional Documentation
- Travel—Staff Only
- Scheduling and Coordination Work
- Management or Supervision
- "Ready for Action" (Idle)

The team spent three weeks walking the halls of the entire hospital. They selected the employees to be observed in order to provide a representative sample of the entire employee population. They looked at nurses, X-ray techs, unit clerks, transport dispatchers, phlebotomists, recovery room aides, admitting clerks, accountants, nursing directors, housekeepers, pharmacists, and everyone else. And the team covered all days of the week and all times of the day and night.

The resulting compilation, weighted by the number of employees in each category, was nothing short of astounding. Jack Stephens and his management team were familiar with the problems with over-specialization, functional organizations, and overly complex processes. But nobody was prepared for what we learned next.

As you can see in Exhibit 36, the biggest consumer of resources within the hospital was documentation. Fully 30% of all labor hours were dedicated to writing stuff down and filing it. Clinical documentation time exceeded clinical work time. Nurses and technicians spent more time documenting what they did than they did doing it. And institutional documentation—admissions paperwork, employee scheduling, time reporting, quality surveys—was almost as bad.

Exhibit 36: LRMC Value-Added Structure

Activity	%
Clinical Documentation	19%
"Ready for Action" (Idle Time)	19%
Scheduling and Coordination	16%
Medical, Technical, and Clinical Work	**14%**
Institutional Documentation	11%
Hotel Services Work	**8%**
Management or Supervision	7%
Transportation - Patient	3%
Transportation - Staff	3%
	100%

Next, 19% of labor costs were a result of being "Ready for Action," or pure idle time. Most of this idle time—85%—was structural in nature, meaning that the staff wasn't lazy; they were simply waiting for something to do. If you are given the job of answering the phone, and you are sitting idle but the phone is not ringing, you are idle through no fault of your own. It is totally due to the way your job was defined. This is known as structural idle time.

Now, as a potential future patient, I like the idea of some structural idle time. My care would likely suffer if all employees were 100% utilized. But 19% seemed like an awfully big number. The staff spent much of their time waiting for something to happen.

Scheduling and coordination time was not surprising to the team. Just look back over the process flow charts and you'll see why. We had the same reaction to transportation time, both staff and patients.

The truly amazing finding was that the hospital devoted only 14% of its resources to activities involved in providing medical, technical, or clinical care to patients. And another 8% on hotel services like housekeeping and food service. In a way, these activities were the only reason why the hospital existed. And yet less than a quarter of its resources were dedicated to them.

The team did analysis in many other areas—the pharmacy formulary, supply prices, repair and maintenance costs, office staffing, and employee benefit costs, to name a few. None of these or other areas appeared to be a major driver of performance, satisfaction, or cost. The nine analyses presented in this chapter formed the basis on which we both defined the problem and developed a solution.

CHAPTER 14

CORE PROBLEMS

Problems are not stop signs, they are guidelines.
—ROBERT H. SCHULLER

The diagnostic analyses just presented do not define a problem or a group of problems. They merely offer facts. Splitting off work from an RN and creating a new position, say a phlebotomist, is neither inherently a good idea nor a bad idea. One cannot use the analytical data to leap to some sort of solution. First, the problem, or in this case problems, must be defined and articulated.

The team synthesized all the analyses and concluded that there were six core problems. All of them were interrelated, and thus, an integrated solution would be required. But for now, the team tried to isolate each problem, and clearly articulate it.

FUNCTIONAL SILOS

The first problem was the functionally siloed organization—defined as departments that do not share information, tools, priorities, and processes with other departments—which completely dominated the organizational structure. There had apparently not been given any thought to organizing around patients or processes, even though that might have made more sense.

The existence of these separate functional organizations was the primary driver of the process complexity that dominated the operations. When an activity spanned several departments, as most did, there was a need for scheduling, coordinating, and work flow handoffs which, by definition, extended the process.

Functional silos also led to an inability to assign accountability for out-comes. In cases where multiple functional organizations were involved in delivering a service, the CEO was the only one with true accountability for the result.

While not a direct result of functional organizations, the silos were a major factor in sub-dividing the work of one position and creating new, lower-paid positions to optimize the skills and training of the higher-paid employee; for example, the creation of an aide position to perform some of the less-skilled duties of the staff RN. Such an arrangement, while seemingly a productivity booster, inevitably led to coordination and com-munication needs that worked against the original intent. Imagine what happened when you created six or eight such positions. The RN became more of a taxi dispatcher than a caregiver.

Perhaps the most significant issue was the lack of focus on the patient! Functional organizations were most concerned with their workloads, staff levels, efficiency, costs, and issues. The patient was someone whom the staff sincerely tried to serve and to provide the best possible care. But the patient was not the entity around which the organization functioned.

COMPARTMENTALIZATION

The medical profession has always pushed for specialization of expertise and jobs. It is no longer enough to be a surgeon, or a cardiac surgeon, or even a cardiac valve surgeon. You need to be a cardiac mitral valve replace-ment surgeon. Some of this is understandable, particularly when it comes to physicians and surgeons; typically, the greater their focus, the greater their expertise and experience.

But by 1986, the healthcare industry had carried specialization too far. Instead of nurses drawing blood, as they had for two hundred years, a new position called a phlebotomist had been developed, whose sole job it was to draw blood. Instead of nurses taking vital signs, as they had for two hun-dred years, a new position called a nurse's aide had been created, whose job it was to take vital signs. Instead of nurses performing a routine incentive spirometry procedure (blow in the tube), as they had for a hundred years, a respiratory therapist who worked in a centrally-dispatched department was now assigned to do this work.

The dictionary defines *specialization* as "the act of devoting oneself to a particular area of occupation or activity"[17] and *compartmentalization* as "the act of dividing into categories, especially to an excessive degree."[18] This perfectly described the jobs and organizations at LRMC in 1986.

The results of all this specialization can be seen in the number of job classifications defined at Lakeland, and the number of FTEs that held each position. In Exhibit 30, we saw that at LRMC, 220 unique positions—39% of the total—had only one full-time employee.

Contrast these compartmentalized jobs, and the specialization implicit in them, with the sort of demand variability that we observed in the last chapter. This was the primary reason that structural idle time (ready for action) accounted for 19% of the value-added structure.

Job compartmentalization was also a major contributing factor in the exceedingly complex processes. The more narrowly jobs are defined, the more people it takes to complete an activity. You can look it up.

Finally, compartmentalization was the primary roadblock to achieving continuity of care; meaning, a relationship with a healthcare professional, like your nurse, who provided the preponderance of your care through time. If continuity was a goal, jobs had to become broader with an expanded scope of responsibilities.

There is a fine line between valuable specialization and burdensome compartmentalization. Provider skill sets can be developed and honed when their work becomes more specialized. But when taken too far, over-specialization leads to job compartmentalization which, in turn, leads to convoluted processes, extreme underutilization, and poor continuity of care. LRMC, and virtually all hospitals at that time, were very much over that line.

PROCESS COMPLEXITY

We saw examples of the extraordinary complexity of two processes in Chapters 5 and 13. The team documented many such flow charts for many LRMC processes. Almost all were protracted and involved many different employees. Given the physical location of centralized ancillary services, many process steps involved transportation of both staff and patients, and,

---

[17] "specialization," Dictionary.reverso.net, 2017, accessed June 2017, www.dictionary.reverso.net

compartmentalization," Dictionary.com, 2017, accessed June 2017, www.dictionary.com.

in turn, the attendant scheduling and coordination tasks.

Clearly, major process simplification would have to be part of any transformative solution. But the nature of the current operation suggested that such simplification would have to be preceded by major changes to the organization, to compartmentalized and specialized job definitions, and even to the physical layout of the hospital. If processes were addressed incrementally, there would be no significant or lasting change.

LABOR/CAPITAL IMBALANCE

In the last chapter, we showed that the annual capital cost of the hospital was 4.8%. Labor costs at Lakeland were 11.9 times greater than capital costs. The labor-capital trade-off was clearly not in balance.

This bias toward lower capital expenditures was clearly the driver of the entire approach to centralized ancillary services, like labs and radiology. And, in turn, it led to the proliferation of specialized, compartmentalized jobs, many of which were involved in scheduling, coordinating, transporting, and documenting. It was a major problem.

EXCESSIVE DOCUMENTATION

You will recall from the value-added structure of LRMC that, on average, 30% of all staff resources in the hospital were used to document. Clinical documentation—nurse's notes, lab results, radiology reports, pharmacy orders, Rx administrations, vital signs charting—accounted for two-thirds of this time. Institutional documentation—admissions paperwork, employee scheduling, time reporting, quality surveys—accounted for the rest.

When you think about this, you quickly realize that this is an untenable and unsustainable situation. Lakeland could not provide increasingly competitive and increasingly sophisticated patient care if caregivers only devoted a fraction of their time to delivering such care, and spent double that time documenting what they did.

Such an environment was not just present among the unit caregiving staff, but within virtually every department in the hospital except food service and housekeeping. This had to change.

DEMAND VARIABILITY

As we saw, the day-to-day variability at the unit or procedure level was very high. In one twenty-five-bed unit, the standard deviation of their daily demand was 6.3. That means that their daily census routinely ranged from twelve to twenty-five. Such variability made it virtually impossible to efficiently staff a patient care unit or a compartmentalized department. This inefficiency was manifested in the high level of structural idle time—19% of the resources were ready for action across the whole organization.

✳

There is a subtle but important difference between the basic analysis of a situation and the definition of a problem. The conditions that drove the operating performance of the hospital—cost, quality, service, and satisfaction—were clearly the result of six factors: (1) functionally-siloed organizations, (2) compartmentalized and overly-specialized jobs, (3) overly-complex processes, (4) an imbalance between labor and capital deployment, (5) excessive documentation, and (6) the variability of patient demand.

There was a great deal of interdependence among and across these problems. Functional organizations and compartmentalized jobs caused processes to be more lengthy and complex. The variability of demand exacerbated the utilization of specialized resources. The imbalance between labor and capital deployment resulted in more job specialization and more extensive documentation requirements.

Understanding these interdependencies became critical when we began to define the transformative solution in Phase II of our work with LRMC.

–PHASE II–

As our findings and conclusions emerged during our Phase I work, we had regularly shared them with LRMC's senior management team. Thus, it was no surprise when the Phase I final report was unanimously endorsed by Jack Stephens and his entire team. Nor were we surprised when they asked us to design a new approach to the delivery of patient care and begin to test it in a thoughtful way. For some time leading up to this point, Jack and I, and my partners John and Phil, had been talking about how to approach this next phase of work.

We all agreed that we needed to design and develop a new operating paradigm and begin to pilot it. There was only one major issue with the Phase II work. We estimated that the work would take six months to complete and that our professional fees would be $800,000. Jack had already invested $500,000 in the Phase I work, which he agreed was well worth the money. But given the localized nature of the hospital industry, if he were to fund Phase II by himself, and if we were to achieve the results we expected to achieve, many other hospitals in the country would end up benefiting from the new approach even though they had not helped to fund the original development. We agreed that this was an issue.

The four of us came up with an unusual solution. We would design and begin to test the new operating paradigm at LRMC, and we would be paid $900,000, not $800,000, to do it. But we would convince five other progressive hospitals from around the country to come along for the ride. They would receive all the findings and conclusions from the Phase I work, and would actively participate in the Phase II effort. They would be invited to attend six day-long progress meetings during the second phase—one each month. They could bring up to three people to each meeting and would have ample opportunity to review the work, engage in discussions, and shape the next steps. The price for admission was $150,000. LRMC was the sixth hospital, and their $150,000 meant that the $900,000 would be fully funded.

Crawford Long Hospital in Atlanta, Vanderbilt University Medical Center in Nashville, St. Vincent's Hospital in Indianapolis, Sentara Healthcare in Norfolk, and Clarkson Hospital in Omaha agreed to join the group. This was an amazing array of successful hospitals that agreed to pay $150,000 to observe, participate, and share in someone else's consulting project. They were true pioneers.

The transformative solution that we developed, with the active participation of all six hospitals, was a radical departure from current practices.

CHAPTER 15

THE TRANSFORMATIVE SOLUTION

When I am working on a problem, I never think about beauty.
I think only how to solve the problem. But when I have finished,
if the solution is not beautiful, I know it is wrong.
—BUCKMINSTER FULLER

Following a kick-off meeting with all six participating hospitals—where we reviewed all of the Phase I work in depth and shared the work plan for Phase II—we went back to work at Lakeland Regional. The team brainstormed various innovative approaches to hospital operations and performed additional analyses to project the cost, quality, and service impacts of these potential solutions.

After several weeks of rigorous work, the team began to home in on the form and structure of a new operating paradigm. This chapter does not recount the various iterations that this development went through. It simply presents our final design. We proposed and defended eight transformative changes which, when done together, would dramatically change the nature of the care delivery system while offering dramatic improvements to the cost, quality, and service outcomes of LRMC. We proposed to change:

1. From functional organizations to operating centers
2. From centralized to unit-based ancillary services
3. From caregivers to care teams
4. From specialized staff to cross-trained staff
5. From care planning to protocols
6. From constant documentation to documentation by exception
7. From historical occupancy to demand forecasting
8. From incidental admissions to master scheduling

OPERATING CENTERS

We first needed to eliminate the functional silos that dominated the existing organization. This was the primary cause of the extensive process complexity and job specialization. We also needed to capitalize on the fact that demand levels began to stabilize once they were aggregated to broader categories—for example, combining neurological, orthopedic, and oncological surgeries into some sort of surgical category. We decided that patients should receive their care in one of five operating centers, which would each share a few key characteristics:

- Needs-Based: The total care needs of patients within each operating center would be very similar in order to tailor its design and increase its focus, quality, and efficiency; e.g., most surgical patients would go in one center.
- Large: To the extent necessary, a center could span multiple geographies so as to take advantage of shared leadership, multi-skilled support, and necessary infrastructure. The size was necessary to dampen daily census variability and, given proper care team design, achieve high levels of staff utilization.
- Self-Contained: Each center would independently deliver the vast majority of services—clinical, technical, administrative, and support—needed by its patients so as to maximize autonomy and eliminate process hand-offs.

This approach allowed LRMC to customize services to meet the needs of more homogenously re-aggregated patient populations with similar demand patterns and care requirements. Typical surgical and medical

Exhibit 37: Generic Difference Between Patient Types

Typical General Surgery Patients		Typical Medical Diagnostic Patients
Short Stay	*Implies*	Long Stay
Schedulable	*Profound*	Usually Not Scheduled
Predictable Care	*Differences*	Unpredictable Care
Low Service Demand	*In Resource*	High Service Demand
Weekday Peak	*Requirements*	Flatter Census Pattern

patients had a profound difference in key aspects of their needs and the characteristics of their stays.

Patients were grouped into five unique operating centers based on their clinical and support needs, as shown in Exhibit 38.

Exhibit 38: Proposed LRMC Patient Centers

Operating Center	Primary Patient Needs	Beds
Diagnostic & Ambulatory Care Center	Testing, Observation & Outpatient Procedures	80
Trauma & Critical Care Center	Stabilization & Treatment	120
Surgical Services Center	Surgery & Recuperation	150
Medical Treatment Center	Health Maintenance & Outplacement	180
Family Wellness Center	Psychological, Emotional & Environmental Care	120
		650

Patient populations within centers were then divided by specialty, and grouped into units. For example:

Exhibit 39: Surgical Services Specialties

Specialty	Projected Census	Unit
Orthopedic Surgery	30	5N
Surgical Oncology	30	5S
Pediatric Surgery	15	5E
Neurosurgery	15	5E
General Surgery	30	5W

Finally, the specialty units had groups of rooms targeted for various sub-specialties, as shown in Exhibit 40.

When incoming patients were admitted, they were first assigned to the appropriate operating center. Demand was stable enough at this level that there was rarely a capacity problem. Then they were assigned to the appropriate specialty unit. Given demand variability, this was possible perhaps

Exhibit 40: Orthopedic Sub-Specialties

Specialty	Projected Census
Knee Replacement	10
Hip Replacement	10
Shoulder Replacement	5
Hand Surgery	3
Ankle Surgery	2
	30

85% of the time. In the example shown above, orthopedic patients were almost always assigned to the orthopedic unit. And then, when feasible, they were assigned to the sub-specialty beds within the unit.

If such an assignment was not possible, at least the patient would be in a surgical center and likely in an orthopedic unit. Cross-trained staff was always available to care for these patients.

REDEPLOYED ANCILLARY SERVICES

We then turned our attention to the centralized ancillary support services, which drove much of the current job compartmentalization and process complexity. We suggested redeploying many of these services with the goal of getting them as close to the patient's bedside as possible.

Most operating units would have their own routine clinical and technical service support capabilities, including:

- Laboratory testing: Basic chemistry, hematology, coagulation, and urinalysis.
- Imaging: Simple chest and extremity diagnostic X-rays.
- Pharmacy: Common meds, narcotics, and IVs.
- Respiratory therapies: Routine bedside treatments.
- Physical therapy: Range of motion exercises.
- Electrodiagnostics: EKGs.

Various staff would be cross-trained, and where necessary, licensed, to perform these basic services. This would also require that capital equipment be purchased for each operating center to enable these unit-based capabilities; for example, a basic X-ray machine for every surgical services unit. These capital expenditures were all easily cost-justified based on the demonstrable labor savings resulting from unit-based capabilities.

Other services remained centralized. But they were organizationally aligned with the center that was the biggest consumer of their capabilities. For example, the Medical Treatment Center was by far the largest user of more complex lab services like microscopy and culturing. Therefore, the remaining central laboratory was part of this center, and services were provided to other centers as required.

One final example of centralized service redeployment: we moved the entire admissions process to the operating centers, the units, and ultimately the bedside. For scheduled procedures, much of the admitting information had already been collected before a patient arrived at the hospital. On the day prior to their procedure, a care team member would call the patient at home, review any pertinent information, and tell them what time to arrive, which unit to report to, and whom to ask for the next day. The patient then reported to their unit, where they were shown to their room and met their caregivers. One of the caregivers completed any outstanding paperwork and the patient was officially admitted. The entire process took ten minutes. For unscheduled admissions, the information gathering took a bit longer, but the patient was still usually admitted within twenty minutes.

CARE TEAMS

Once we had defined the five operating centers and deployed basic ancillary services to each one, we were able to move the preponderance of patient care back to the unit. This allowed us to address the issues of compartmentalization, structural idle time, and process complexity. We struck on the idea of Care Pairs as being the primary deliverers of bedside patient care. Each pair would include an RN and a tech, at least one of whom would be cross-trained and licensed to perform 90%+ of the care required by a specific patient population. Many of these Care Pair teammates had been lab or radiology techs prior to the reorganization, and were already licensed to perform some procedures on the unit.

In some cases, a Care Trio, with one RN and two techs, or vice versa, made more sense. That was perfectly okay too if it was appropriate to meet the needs of a specific patient population and achieved high levels of resource utilization.

We developed the concept of the Care Pair as a self-directed work team. That meant that while the RN was the nominal team leader, patient care would usually be provided by whichever team member was available. Each Care Pair divided and shared the work basically on a real-time basis. Obviously, some things required an RN license to perform—passing medications and performing assessments. But all the rest of the work was shared between the pair. If the RN was busy, the tech would put the patient in a wheelchair, take them down the hall to the radiology room, take an X-ray, and take the patient back to their bed. If the tech was busy, the RN would take the X-ray, assuming that both were licensed.

Literally, 90%+ of the clinical and technical patient care and support was provided by a self-directed Care Pair. They didn't need permission; they didn't need to be scheduled; they didn't need to be supervised. Each pair just delivered the care to four, or possibly five, patients.

We then linked the Care Pairs across shifts and days of the week. LRMC adopted a radically new approach to scheduling caregiving resources. There were three shifts of weekday employees who worked either 7 a.m. to 3 p.m., 3 p.m. to 11 p.m., or 11 p.m. to 7 a.m., Monday through Friday. They were paid for forty hours per week, received full benefits, and yes, they were off every weekend. The weekends were staffed on two twelve-hour shifts on Saturday and Sunday. Weekend staff were paid for forty hours, even though they only worked twenty-four, but they did not receive any benefits.

This meant that Lakeland could link the Care Pairs on each different shift. Three weekday Care Pairs and two weekend Care Pairs could provide 24/7 care for their assigned patients, as shown in Exhibit 41.

Exhibit 41: Care Pair Deployment

	Mon	Tue	Wed	Thu	Fri	Sat	Sun
M-F Day Shift	AB	AB	AB	AB	AB		
M-F Evening Shift	CD	CD	CD	CD	CD		
M-F Night Shift	EF	EF	EF	EF	EF		
Weekend Day Shift						GH	GH
Weekend Night Shift						IJ	IJ

Remember the Faces in the Parade exhibit? Forty-six different nursing, support, and transport staff interacted with a patient over a typical four-day stay. With linked Care Pairs, that could be reduced to as low as ten for some short-stay patients, or as high as fifteen for stays of one week or more. This provided a major boost to the continuity of care.

CROSS-TRAINING

A key enabler of the new approach would become LRMC's ability to cross-train, and when necessary, license the RNs and techs that comprised the patient care delivery team. The hospital worked with a local community college to develop curricula for various clinical training, and encouraged and paid for the staff to attend these classes.

The staff was very motivated to broaden their skill base after Jack Stephens announced his intention to develop a new compensation system for direct caregivers. Historically, this staff had been paid based on educational level and tenure. A nurse with a master's degree would be paid more than a nurse with an associate degree. One who had been employed for ten years would make more than one who had been employed for two years.

In the future, the sole basis of compensation for the clinical staff would become skills mastered, demonstrated, and if necessary, licensed. A brand-new RN with an associate degree and no additional training in X-ray, lab, or physical therapy might make $20 per hour or $40,000 per year. An RN with a master's degree who was qualified to care for a wide range of patient types, and was licensed to take X-rays and perform lab tests, might be paid $50 per hour or $100,000 per year. LRMC paid for skills, capabilities, and flexibility.

Let's come back to our orthopedics unit, 5 North. A brand-new RN might be assigned to work with an experienced RN as part of a Care Pair for two weeks, caring for knee replacement patients. Then the RN would be paired with a tech, and continue to be focused on knee replacements whenever possible. Another RN on the unit might be experienced in hip, knee, and shoulder replacements. Her Care Pair could be assigned as needed across several sub-specialties to meet varying demand patterns.

CLINICAL PROTOCOLS

Nurses had historically developed a handwritten care plan for each patient under their care. While this was relatively easy to do for common procedures and conditions, it definitely contributed to the excessive amount of time spent on clinical documentation. This had to change.

The dictionary defines a *protocol* as "the plan for carrying out a patients' treatment regimen."[19] In 1986, there were no documented protocols for the many conditions treated and procedures performed at LRMC, even though many were treated and performed frequently, and the care required and expected patient outcomes were virtually the same.

Take a straightforward procedure like heart bypass surgery. Patients entered the hospital during the afternoon prior to the procedure. Every patient's pre-operative care was virtually the same: EKGs, chest X-rays, food service, vital signs on the day of arrival; and lab work, vital signs, and a sedative on the morning of surgery. Post-operatively, the same uniformity of care was apparent: four days of inpatient recovery, vital signs taken every two hours, a set of medications for blood thinning and pain, and so on.

It was just that no one had written down the work tasks required or the outcomes expected. The specification of some treatments was written, as in the case of Rx orders. But other tasks were communicated verbally, and passed on from caregiver to caregiver. And each patient required their own care plan.

This resulted in a copious amount of clinical documentation. Nurses, techs, and unit clerks had to plan and record every discrete element of the care process. We had to find a better way if we were to achieve any major improvements to the value-added structure.

The hospital needed to develop protocols for every procedure or treatment it offered. These protocols would specify all the elements of care in a time-phased sequence, and the range of outcomes that were expected. They would include all bedside nursing activities and all routinely prescribed medications, lab tests, and X-ray procedures. They would be presented in four-hour time blocks for the patient's entire projected length of stay.

Exhibit 42 shows a simplistic example of what two steps in a cardiac post-operative protocol might look like.

---

[19] "protocol," Dictionary.com, 2017, accessed April 2017, www.dictionary.com.

Exhibit 42: Example of a Post-Op Cardiac Protocol

1. Assess upon arrival from post-op:
   - blood pressure
   - heart rate and rhythm
   - O2 saturation by pulse oximeter (SpO2)
   - temperature
   - pulses in all 4 extremities
   - respiratory rate
   - pain level
   - CVP, PA pressures, CO, CI, SVR
   - SvO2
   - vasoactive/inotropic drip concentrations
2. Assess every 15 minutes x 4, every 30 minutes x 2, then every 2 hours:
   - blood pressure
   - heart rate
   - heart rhythm
   - respiratory rate
   - oxygen saturation

As we implemented the patient-focused hospital, the most time-consuming activity was the creation of clinical protocols. They were primarily drafted by experienced nurses, but then they were reviewed many times by other RNs, doctors, and various technical staff. The protocols were then loaded into a newly developed system: The Automated Case Manager.

DOCUMENTATION BY EXCEPTION

Based on the envisioned availability of protocols for every procedure or treatment offered, we developed a concept called documentation by exception, whereby the caregiver would only document exceptions to these expected norms.

For example, when our heart bypass patient was returned to the cardiac surgery unit, the care team was instructed through the protocol to take the patient's vital signs. The acceptable range of possible outcomes might have been a blood pressure of 90/60 to 140/90, and a temperature between 95.0 and 101.1. If the patient's vital signs were within those ranges, no documentation was required (or permitted).

But if they were outside of these acceptable ranges, they would be documented, and if appropriate, the physician would be notified.

Exhibit 43 shows the addition to the protocol presented in the last section after it was broadened to incorporate documentation by exception:

Exhibit 43: Documentation & Notification Addition to Post-Op Cardiac Protocol

3. Document & notify M.D. of the following results:
- cardiac index <2 L/min/m2
- MAP <60 or >90 mmHg.
- SBP >140 mmHg of < 90mmHg.
- SvO2 <60%
- cardiac dysrhythmias
- temperature =35° or >38.5° C (95° or >101.1° F)
- chest tube & JP drainage >100 mL/hr. x 2 hours

This documentation process was also part of the Automated Case Study system. This system was also linked to the pharmacy, lab, and radiology systems so that an integrated patient record could be created and maintained.

DEMAND FORECASTING

LRMC had never really done sophisticated demand forecasting. They looked at historical seasonality. They identified trends. They used common sense. But given the random nature of many admissions—and given the fact that demand was only captured for the twenty-six patient care units and for the hospital in total, and not for surgical or medical specialties or sub-specialties—it was only possible to project total hospital occupancy with any degree of accuracy.

With the new operating center organizational structure and the designation of various specialty and sub-specialty disciplines within each center, better and more actionable demand forecasting was now within reach.

We began with operating center demand projections. The fact that four of the units contained more than one hundred beds made the demand data statistically significant over virtually any time horizon. We designed and developed a system to forecast overall center demand by day, week, and month on a rolling basis for the next twelve months.

This showed, for example, the day-of-the-week bias of surgical services demand—weekdays high, weekends low, and the seasonal bias of medical treatment demand—caused by flu season, allergy season, and the like.

Then we tried to forecast specialty demand, such as orthopedic surgery, neurosurgery, surgical oncology, and general surgery within the surgical services center. The historical demand for most specialties had statistical significance, but only at the monthly and annual levels. This was still helpful in developing appropriate staffing plans and calculating the overall number of Care Pairs required through time in a center.

At the sub-specialty level, like hips, knees, and shoulders in orthopedics, the data would only support annual demand forecasts. The day-to-day and week-to-week variabilities were so extreme as to make any monthly or weekly demand forecasts meaningless.

However, such annual projections were valuable in sizing the designated sub-specialty areas within a given unit. For example, within the thirty-bed orthopedics unit, 50% of the beds might be earmarked for knee replacement and 30% for hip replacement. This was also key information for determining the number of Care Pairs required on the unit and their optimal training, experience, and qualifications.

The inherent randomness of many hospital admissions made demand forecasting very difficult. Staffing on each center and unit had to be made adaptive to ever-changing circumstances. But these demand forecasts went a long way in easing this burden.

MASTER SCHEDULING

Each operating center needed a planner/scheduler to forecast demand, and to develop staffing and deployment plans to meet these demands, while at the same time achieving acceptable levels of resource utilization. This was a key new position for the hospital.

The Surgical Services Center, and to a lesser extent the Family Wellness Center, which included OB/GYN and maternity, presented an opportunity to take scheduling to a higher level. Much of the demand in these two centers was non-emergent, which means that it could be scheduled in advance.

Surgical services patients, and their surgeons, required an operating room, a patient room, and a Care Pair. Each of these posed a possible capacity constraint, and a more sophisticated approach to scheduling would enable better resource utilization.

One of our teammates, Bill Leander, developed an automated Master Scheduling System, which considered all these resource constraints simultaneously. Then, for the first six months following implementation, Bill served in the new position of Master Scheduler.

When a doctor's office called requesting a surgery date for a non-emergent patient, Bill would enter the patient's name and surgical procedure. The system would look at the available capacity of the ORs, unit and subspecialty beds, the unit Care Pairs, and the surgeon's preferred schedule, and would suggest a date for admission and an OR time. If the surgeon's office pushed for an earlier date, the system would alert Bill to projected capacity problems, allowing him to make informed judgments about whether to acquiesce to the surgeon's request or not. If, for example, a hip replacement patient ended up on a general surgery unit, no problem. But if a knee replacement patient would have to be treated on an oncology unit, that request could not be accommodated.

Demand forecasting and master scheduling both became major enablers of effective resource deployment, and both contributed greatly to improvements in staff utilization and continuity of care.

Ultimately, as I said at the start of this chapter, the core problems of LRMC were interdependent, and the design of the patient-focused hospital was iterative and non-linear. The transformative solution that we developed was multi-layered and the elements of it were very interdependent. To summarize:

- Care delivery resources were organized into five unique operating units, which were defined based on the similarity of patient care needs.
- Higher-volume ancillary and support services, such as radiology, pathology, physical therapy, and admissions, were physically redeployed to the units of each operating center.
- Care Pairs were established as the primary resource for the delivery of bedside patient care. They were cross-trained and licensed

so that they could deliver 90%+ of the care for an assigned group of medical or surgical specialty and sub-specialty patients.

- Protocols were developed for every procedure of every patient type. These formed the basis of a new approach to creating the patient record: documentation by exception.
- Finally, demand forecasting systems were developed to drive the resource staffing and deployment plans of each center and unit. And master schedulers were put in place to manage this process.

The new organization chart, shown in Exhibit 44, demonstrates the new focus on patients and integrated patient care.

Exhibit 44: Patient-Focused Organization

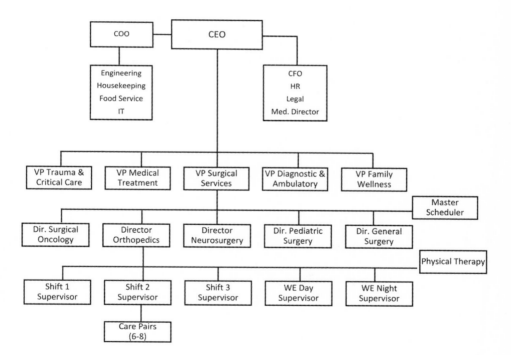

—PHASE III—

At the end of Phase II, three of the participants were eager to begin to pilot the concept. We and they agreed to continue with the monthly review meetings so that each participant could learn from the others. We would also work independently with each of the three hospitals to help them design pilot programs, develop protocols, train the staff, and test the new operations strategy. Our fees from each would be enough to provide ample resources to allow us to continue to organize and lead the monthly group meetings.

Gary Shows, Adam Zauder, Bill Leander, and I, as well as my two healthcare partners, John Smith and Phil Lathrop, continued to form the core team from Booz Allen. But at this point, Lakeland began to assign a number of people to the pilot implementation effort. These folks would assist in the design, and then would become the first staff members to actually work in a patient-focused hospital. They, too, were real pioneers.

CHAPTER 16

IMPLEMENTATION

Be creative while inventing ideas, but be disciplined
while implementing them.
—AMIT KALANTRI

L RMC aggressively approached piloting and implementing the new operating concept. One of the five new operating centers would be called
Surgical Services, wherein all general surgery patients would be grouped
to receive their pre- and post-operative care. We selected one of the units
that would ultimately be a part of the center, and designed and implemented a pilot program. As I remember, this unit initially was composed
of twenty beds, but it was quickly expanded to forty beds. Ultimately, the
center would be comprised of 150 beds.

Prior to the actual implementation, we spent three months working
with the doctors and clinical staff to develop and document protocols for
every surgical procedure that would be assigned to this unit. We modified
the physical space to accommodate basic X-ray machines, mini-labs, and
a satellite pharmacy.

We designed new jobs and developed new job descriptions, and we
offered existing clinical staff the chance to be a part of the pilot. Those who
were uncomfortable were assigned to other units. Those who chose to be
pioneers were provided with extensive training, and obtained licenses to
provide various clinical procedures and services.

We developed an integrated scheduling system that considered bed capacity, care team capacity, operating room availability, and physician pref-
erences to optimize the utilization of these four capacity constraints and
allow physicians to easily schedule their elective surgeries, while providing

continuity of clinical care for the patients. We also created, filled, and trained a new position titled Master Scheduler to manage the system and have overall accountability for scheduling patients into and out of the unit, and for the resulting continuity of care, staff and bed utilization, and physician satisfaction.

Then the surgical services pilot became fully operational, and almost from the beginning, it ran smoothly. Some tweaks to the design were implemented, but in large part, the center worked almost exactly as we envisioned.

While all of this was going on, we worked with management to prepare for the design, development, and implementation of four additional operating units. The transformation continued for several years, although our direct involvement began to be reduced as management took over more and more of the leadership challenge.

This change initiative and its implementation spanned some six years and challenged almost all the conventional wisdom about operations management in hospitals. It was, without question, change agency at its best: extensive, strategic, and ground-breaking. It was the highlight of my professional career.

CHAPTER 17

THE RESULTS

Normal people attempt countless goals with limited success. Weird people focus on just one God-given objective with tremendous results.
—Craig Groeschel

The transformative solution that we arrived at during Phase II called for eliminating functionally-based organizations in favor of operating centers, resourced to provide 95% of the care and support to its designated patient populations. We recommended decentralizing several key ancillary services, and proposed putting X-ray machines, basic lab equipment, and a satellite pharmacy in all centers and most patient units. We proposed the concept of care teams that could directly deliver at least 90% of the care to an assigned group of four or five patients. We suggested developing written protocols for every Diagnostic-Related Group (DRG) procedure and recommended a new policy of documentation by exception.

By now, you should be able to imagine the magnitude of the benefits that Lakeland Regional Medical Center was able to achieve. Given the level of detail I presented in the last few chapters, I won't dwell on the drivers of the results presented here.

CLINICAL EFFICACY

We begin with the most important result: clinical efficacy, or the ability to achieve desired clinical outcomes for patients.

- Readmission rates for the same diagnosis or post-surgical complications and infections declined, likely because of fewer faces in the parade and improved continuity of patient care.

- The number of medication errors declined dramatically, likely because of the satellite pharmacies and the improved continuity of care.
- The number of patient incidents, such as falls, declined, likely because of patients being better oriented to their environment and receiving greater continuity of care.
- The length of stay declined up to 15% for all surgical center patients, likely because of the standardized care protocols and the continuity of care provided.
- Post-operative temperature spikes declined among patients in the new surgery center. It was felt that this was due to quicker post-operative respiratory therapies administered directly by the care team.

There were many other comparative measures of patient outcomes in the newly restructured operating centers. All of them either showed improvement, which was at times significant, or showed no change. There was never an instance of outcome degradation.

LABOR COSTS

Labor costs declined significantly. In Chapter 13, we pointed out that historical labor costs had been 57.2% of total costs. The labor costs of the new patient-focused model were 47.9%, a 16.3% reduction. This was clearly a result of reorganizing and redeploying resources, of redefining jobs and authorities, and of streamlining processes. And the additional fixed assets required to accomplish this only increased capital costs from 5% to 6%.

We saw similar reductions to the relative cost of labor at other hospitals that implemented the patient-focused paradigm during the 1990s.

CONSTITUENT SATISFACTION

By all measures, the patients were thrilled with this new model of care. Satisfaction scores, as measured by a Press Ganey survey, the standard for the industry, showed uniform and dramatic improvements.

One unit in the Medical Treatment Center went from being the most poorly rated unit in the hospital to being the highest-rated unit in its first month of operation.

Physician reaction was a bit more diverse. All the doctors liked the higher level of care provided by the care teams and the quicker availability of routine diagnostic test results. But the new approach necessitated some major changes in physician behavior, such as adapting to the new master scheduling system and getting used to the concept of documentation by exception. Some doctors resisted this change. And a few were vocal about it. It's interesting that the biggest complainers were doctors with the lowest admission rates. The high-volume admitters all got behind the program very quickly.

The staff was also very pleased with the new operating model. Predictably, they loved the new sense of empowerment, the positive feedback from patients, the many streamlined processes, and especially the new approach to documentation. The weekday/weekend shift option was a big hit. Turnover was astonishingly low on the restructured units, although at the time, it was unclear if this would be sustainable.

VALUE-ADDED STRUCTURE

The most striking impact of the patient-focused restructuring was its resulting value-added structure. Once the restructuring was in place, the team once again walked the halls of the units and captured the activities engaged in by selected employees at the moment they were seen. We had to make some adjustments because most ancillary services remained centralized pending the conversions of other units and centers. Exhibit 45 shows that the results were still indicative of a major transformation.

Exhibit 45: Post-Restructuring Value-Added Structure

Value Category	Old %	New %
Medical, Technical, and Clinical	14%	36%
Hotel Services	8%	13%
"Ready for Action" (Idle)	19%	12%
Clinical Documentation	19%	11%
Scheduling and Coordination	16%	9%
Institutional Documentation	11%	8%
Management or Supervision	7%	7%
Transportation - Patient	3%	2%
Transportation - Staff	3%	2%
	100%	100%

Whereas before, the primary focus of the hospital staff had been on documenting and scheduling activities, and waiting for them to happen, the focus was clearly now on patient care. Resources devoted to direct patient care were double those of hospitals using the conventional operating approach. There was still adequate structural idle time to deal with emergent and variable demand. But the resources devoted to documentation, scheduling, coordinating, and transportation showed significant decreases.

It was a privilege and an honor to lead this initiative. It certainly drew on absolutely all the change management experience of the entire Booz Allen team. And it required creative yet disciplined thought to envision the new operating paradigm.

Jack Stephens and his entire management team also had to embrace change and accept challenges to the conventional order. They, too, were challenged to be creative and adaptive. Perhaps most of all, they had to have the courage to confront an industry. There were many times when their peers thought they had lost their minds. But they persevered. They have my profound respect and admiration.

Here is a final story that was told to me by Bain Farris, the then-CEO of St. Vincent's Hospital in Indianapolis. Bain was one of the participants in the LRMC consortium, and began to aggressively implement the patient-focused approach in 1989.

It seems that one day Bain was walking down the hall of a newly restructured operating center in the hospital. He was stopped by a gentleman, who said: "Aren't you the CEO here?"

"That, I am. I'm Bain Farris."

"Well, I've got a complaint," said the gentleman. "I don't appreciate being lied to!"

"Who lied to you?" Bain asked.

"Both my doctor and my nurse have lied to me this morning," he said. "They told me that my mother would not need to go to intensive care following her surgery; and yet here she is."

"I don't understand," Bain replied. "This is not an intensive care unit. It is an orthopedic surgery unit. Nobody lied to you."

"That can't be true," said the increasingly frustrated man. "There have been nurses and technicians in and out of her room non-stop since she got back from surgery. Someone is with her almost all the time."

"Let me explain," Bain said with a smile. "We recently implemented a new approach to delivering patient care in the hospital, and we have two trained caregivers assigned to your mother and three other patients in nearby rooms. They are responsible for virtually all of your mother's care—they take vital signs, they pass medications, they take X-rays, they do lab tests, they do virtually everything—and one of them should be with your mother almost all of the time immediately after she comes back from surgery."

"That's amazing!" the gentleman said. "And here I thought that she was in intensive care."

The patient-focused hospital was a revolutionary approach to delivering patient care. God bless the pioneers who were part of its development.

FOLLOWING UP

*There is nothing more difficult to take in hand, more perilous
to conduct, or more uncertain in its success, than to take the lead
in the introduction of a new order of things.*
—Niccolo Machiavelli

I have resisted writing about the sustainability of the change initiatives discussed in this book. First, I didn't want to get bogged down in more, and potentially distracting, information. Second, I didn't want the client's inability to implement to detract from the learning potential of the case study. Third, it has been twenty to thirty years since many of these changes took place. I have long since lost touch with the people and the companies. I have no idea what most of them are doing today.

That said, I have revisited five of the companies about whom I've written case studies in this book, and tried to determine if the improvements that we recommended have endured. It is a mixed bag of results.

TARGET STORES

In Chapter 11, I reviewed the supply chain management work that we did for Target Stores back in the 1980s. Due to the very slow sales volume of many SKUs at the individual store level, their existing, highly efficient distribution system imposed severe inefficiencies and cost penalties on each store.

We turned the whole thing on its head. Distribution was charged with replenishing the stores daily, and replacing the actual sales quantities. If the store sold two bottles of shampoo, the warehouse sent two bottles of shampoo. And if the stores were open seven days a week, so were the warehouses.

While distribution costs increased significantly, the net savings to the company were sizeable, due to less inventory, less shrinkage, lower store labor costs, and fewer stock-outs.

This morning, I called the store manager at my local Target. I asked him only two questions, and determined that Target has reverted to an efficient distribution system, undoubtedly resulting in greater store labor expenses. First, I asked him if they received replenishment orders on slow-moving items in case pack quantities. He reported that they frequently received case pack replenishments on low-volume items, and when there was not room to store the entire case on the shelf, they returned the box to the back room, a process that seemingly has now become a verb: *to back-store.*

Then I asked him about the frequency of warehouse shipments. He reported that the store received maybe five trucks a week, although, he said, it is a high-volume store. Other stores, he said, received only two or three trucks per week. He also told me that distribution had recently piloted an approach of using smaller trucks and shipping full truckloads to stores more frequently. But, he said: "They couldn't make the economics work."

Sometimes, a successfully implemented change initiative doesn't sustain. It is simply the nature of the beast. If you can, try to convince yourself that if all problems got solved once and for all, there wouldn't be anything for tomorrow's change agents to do. Who knows? Target Stores may become fertile ground for someone reading this book.

CADILLAC

In Chapter 4, I discussed the work that we did for Cadillac in 1989. We started out assessing the effectiveness of their marketing programs. However, as we analyzed the data, we learned that the average age of their customers was increasing by more than a year each year. Their customers were dying off. We concluded that the problem was not with their marketing; it was with their products and their quality. Cadillac had ceased to appeal to younger generations.

It turned out that our concerns were on the mark. But the management team was entrenched and change-resistant. It wasn't until fourteen years later, in 2003, that Cadillac finally introduced the CTS Sedan to try to appeal to younger buyers, and to try to restore their brand, their reputation, and their market share.

Unfortunately for Cadillac, our work and their reaction was too little, too late. Total Cadillac sales in 2016 were 170,000—only 56% of their 1986 sales level.[20] Here is the real sadness in this situation. In 1986, Cadillac was the

---

[20] "Chrysler US Car Sales Figures," Carsalesbase.com, accessed October 2017, www.carsalesbase.com/us-car-sales-data/chrysler/.

number one seller of luxury cars in the United States. Lexus hadn't even been launched. And Mercedes, BMW, and Audi were not dominant players. Today, Lexus, Mercedes, and BMW each have a 15%+ share of the U.S. luxury car market. Audi has 10%. And Cadillac is now in fifth place with an 8% share.[21] They lost their way in the eighties and nineties and have never recovered.

That should be a lesson for every company. Cadillac was an iconic brand. They had been around since 1902. They defined and owned the luxury car market in the U.S. for over eighty years. But they got complacent and lost their edge. And they haven't recovered. Given the global competitiveness of today's luxury car market, it is highly unlikely that they ever will.

NORWEGIAN CRUISE LINE

In Chapter 12, I discussed pricing and suggested that many companies leave a lot of money on the table due to sub-optimal pricing strategies. One of the examples I cited involved Norwegian Caribbean Cruise Line, now simply known as Norwegian Cruise Line or NCL.

Based on our analysis, we suggested that within a reasonable range, price had no measurable effect on demand. An economist would say that there was complete price inelasticity for one-week Caribbean cruises priced from $1,200 to $1,500 per person. Once the decision to take a Caribbean cruise had been made, the ship and the itinerary, not the price, apparently drove the ultimate purchase decision.

We recommended that NCCL raise their prices to the top of the competitive range, which they did. For the next year, the company experienced no decrease in demand and saw revenues rise by almost 15%.

Just today, I went online and researched cruise pricing among the four largest competitors: NCL, Carnival, Royal Caribbean, and Holland America. Damned if NCL hasn't stayed the course. I checked pricing for a balcony cabin on a seven-day cruise of the Western Caribbean on various dates over the next eighteen months.

There are very likely to be other factors at work here. But it does appear that NCL has maintained an aggressive pricing policy, as shown in Exhibit 46.

---

[21] "Luxury Car Market Share: United States 2016 Statistic," Statista.com, accessed October 2017, www.statista.com/statistics/287620/luxury-vehicles-united-states-premium-vehicle-market-share/.

Exhibit 46: Current Cruise Prices

	12/17	2/18	12/18
NCL	$999	$1,129	$899
Holland America	$899	$999	
Carnival	$899	$999	
RCCL	$759		$729

GENERAL MOTORS

In Chapter 11, we reviewed the pervasive cost of complexity in the automotive industry. Using the 1985 Chevy Monte Carlo as a test case, we quantified complexity costs for a range of build configuration possibilities. Referring again to Exhibit 16, the resulting complexity cost curve was most enlightening:

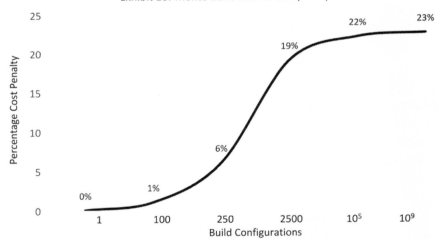

Exhibit 16: Monte Carlo Cost of Complexity

This analysis showed for the first time that the cost of complexity in a typical GM car was 23% of the total cost of the car, at that time perhaps $1,500 to $2,000.

We did this work for George Peables, the CEO of General Motors of Canada. But it was the General Managers in Detroit who controlled all the product offerings for their divisions: Chevrolet, Oldsmobile, Buick, Pontiac, and Cadillac. The only General Manager that we could get to understand the implications of these findings and act on them was Ed Mertz, the GM of Buick. He launched several simplification initiatives which, over a few years, dramatically reduced the build configurations of all Buick models.

Just today, I went online and researched three comparable car models—one from Chevy, one from Honda, and one from Buick—to determine their build configurations today. The results, shown in Exhibit 47, were surprising.

Exhibit 47: Current Build Configurations

	Chevy Malibu	Honda Accord	Buick Verano
Trim Levels	5	7	3
Drive Trains	3	2	1
Colors	9	8	4
Interiors	4	3	3
Packages	3	0	5
Options	16	5	0
Build Configurations	25,920	1,680	180
Minimum MSRP	$22,555	$22,445	$21,065

Chevrolet has made great progress in simplifying their offering. But they are still missing the boat. The Monte Carlo, which was discontinued in 2007, had 10^9 possible ways to assemble the car. The Chevy Malibu is down to 25,920. Unfortunately, if you look at the cost curve, you will see that complexity cost doesn't begin to dramatically decline until you reach 2,500 build configurations. Chevy's manufacturing costs are seemingly still significantly driven by complexity.

Honda, on the other hand, has increased the complexity of their Accord model. In 1985, the Accord had only 240 build configurations. Now it has 1,680. The consumer choices on a Honda Accord are still relatively limited. But Honda does seem to be moving in the wrong direction.

Now look at Buick. The vision and leadership of Ed Mertz apparently lives on. The Buick Verano, a direct competitor of the Accord and the Malibu, has only 180 build configurations. Buick is only incurring a 1% to 2%

complexity cost penalty, while their competitors are being penalized by 15% to 20%. Said another way, Buick chooses to spend money on technology and quality, rather than pissing it away trying to cope with complexity.

I am persuaded that the roughly $1,500 price advantage that Buick has over two large competitors is largely a result of their discipline in holding the line on available trim levels, colors, and free-standing options.

PATIENT-FOCUSED HOSPITALS

I have not kept pace with the goings-on at Lakeland Regional Medical Center. I'm sure that Jack Stephens and his management team are long-since retired. And I don't remember any executive in the early 1990s who was poised to take over as CEO.

But I have kept up with St. Vincent's Hospital in Indianapolis. They seem to have continued to evolve as a patient-focused hospital. Here are two excerpts from their website.

ST. VINCENT ORTHOPEDIC CENTER
Specialized clinical teams and focused care combine with leading-edge technology to build a proven record in successful outcomes

ST. VINCENT WOMEN'S CENTER
Dedicated to providing the highest level of specialized and comprehensive medical care exclusively for women through every stage of life

St. Vincent's was named a Leapfrog Group Top Hospital in 2012. It was the only Indiana hospital on the list. The Top Hospital designation is the most competitive national hospital quality award in the country. Winners are selected from nearly 1,200 hospitals that publicly report performance in three critical areas: how patients fare; resources used to care for patients; and management practices that promote safety and quality.

Finally, I've been hospitalized five times in three different facilities over the past six years. And I've seen evidence of the use and acceptance of patient-focused principles. Although they didn't call them that, they all used Care Pairs to deliver bedside care. And all of them claimed to use protocols and seemingly documented by exception. I also saw some evidence of operating center-like approaches.

Last winter, I had shoulder replacement surgery at a hospital in Naples,

Florida. Winter is a busy time in south Florida, and the hospital was 100% occupied. I awoke in post-op at about three o'clock in the afternoon, and then waited for over five hours for a bed to become available. Shortly after eight o'clock, I was moved to a room on the orthopedic unit on the 4th floor. After my RN introduced herself and her tech (yes, they were a Care Pair!), I asked her to help me adjust my sling.

"I don't have much experience with slings," she said. "This unit normally houses knee replacement patients."

"No problem," I said. "I had my other shoulder replaced two years ago, so I can show you how to adjust it."

"Thanks," she said.

"So, I'm in a knee replacement unit?" I continued.

"Yes," she responded. "The shoulder unit is at the other end of the floor, but it's fully occupied tonight, so they put you here. Don't worry," she added. "You'll still get excellent care."

And I did. This seemed to be a page right out of the patient-focused playbook. It felt like an operating center and it felt like cross-trained Care Pairs. And for a one-day stay, there were only about fifteen faces in the parade.

FINIS

Of the twelve coaching points illustrated in *Corporate Goad,* the ones concerned with attracting and developing talent, getting their attention, and leading them from the front may be the most important. Certainly, if you fail to do this, the opportunities outlined in the later chapters will never come to pass. Therefore, I have chosen to bring the book to an end by sharing a few more stories, each of them illustrative of one of the team-building challenges presented early in the book. They are meant to simply reinforce my observations and counsel about becoming an effective agent of change, and perhaps, entertain you a bit.

As I described in Chapter 1, successful change agency begins with finding and recruiting talent. In 1981, I had been with Booz Allen for two years. I traveled virtually every week, and had a regular taxi driver that I scheduled in advance to take me to and from the airport. His name was Tim Dunn. Two of my colleagues, Bob Howe and Paul Branstad, also used Tim for airport trips, and if we were going out at roughly the same times, we would double or triple up at Tim's suggestion. Each of us enjoyed challenging debates and conversations about a wide range of topics with Tim on our ways to and from the airport.

I remember one conversation that Tim initiated when we were discussing counter-intuitive findings. It seems that during World War II, a statistician was asked to help the RAF decide where to add armor to their bombers to hopefully reduce the chances that they would be shot down. He ultimately recommended that they add more armor to the places where there had been no damage in the sample of otherwise shot-up aircraft.

The statistician, Tim said, only had data on the planes that had returned to Britain, so the bullet holes that he saw were all in places where a plane could be hit and still survive. The planes that were shot down must have been hit in different places than those that returned, so he recommended adding armor to the places where the surviving planes were lucky enough not to have been hit.

I had never had, nor have I had since, such conversations in a taxi. Tim was a very intelligent, thoughtful, and worldly cab driver.

One day when I was working in the office, Bob Howe stopped by to talk. "I think that Timmy is one smart guy," he offered.

"I agree," I said. "He's got a degree from Case Western in English Literature, and I think that he graduated magna cum laude. Plus our conversations are off the scale."

"Let's hire him," Bob said. "Paul agrees that he's one of the smartest guys he's ever met."

"You've got my vote," I said.

Bob arranged for Tim to visit the office and scheduled ten staff and partners to interview him. The decision to hire him was unanimous, and two weeks later, Tim, a recent full-time taxi driver, joined Booz Allen as a Research Associate. Tim had a successful five-year stint at the firm, and, I believe, went on to enjoy a good career in business. Talent pops up in unusual places.

One of the key coaching points I discussed in Chapter 3 was the need to, from time to time, get people's attention. In 1980, I was part of a team that did some very progressive manufacturing strategy work for Deere & Company, the large farm machinery manufacturer based in Moline, Illinois. While we had clearly articulated the work that was necessary and that we intended to do in our proposal, many of the manufacturing executives did not appreciate how much of a departure from earlier manufacturing planning efforts this work would be. It definitely involved some new analytical approaches and challenged conventional wisdom about the manufacturing function.

About six weeks after we began, we decided to hold a progress meeting with our client, Jim Lardner, who was Deere's Senior Vice President of Manufacturing and Engineering, and his senior staff, about twenty people in all. As the project manager of this assignment, it fell to me to draft the report, and then, after heavy editing by the Officer-in-Charge, Bob Mayer, to finalize it. I was also the one who would present the material to the client.

On the fateful day, I began to present the results of our work to date. Shortly after I began, various executives in the room began to challenge me.

"What in the hell does that mean?" "Why are you doing that?" "This isn't what we hired you to do!"

This went on for twenty minutes, at which time Bob Mayer spoke up: "Jim," Bob said to Mr. Lardner, "you guys paid a lotta money for this stuff. Why don't you shut the hell up and listen? You might just learn something!"

"You're right, Bob," Jim replied. "Shut up, guys; and go on, Kurt."

I continued my presentation, and by the end of it, most of the audience had come around and could see the value in our approach. Bob Mayer became my hero that morning. I would have followed him off the edge of the earth. But all he really did was get their attention.

The pricing analysis that we did for Norwegian Caribbean Cruise Line was just one element of the work that we did for them. Much of our operations work was conducted aboard a ship, as that was the product and that was where virtually all of the expenses were incurred.

A few days after we were awarded the assignment, the team went on a three-day, roundtrip weekend cruise from Miami to Nassau to begin to familiarize ourselves with Caribbean cruising. Not surprisingly, when the officers and crew learned of our remit and our presence, they were wary. Some of the wariness manifested itself as outright threats against our well-being.

It was about ten o'clock on the night we left Miami, and I was walking alone on one of the outside decks. An officer, who turned out to be the Chief Engineer, the second highest ranking officer on the ship, approached me. "Aren't you one of those management consultants?" he asked.

"Yes, I am," I replied.

"Well, I hope that you and your team are strong swimmers," he said, while gesturing over the railing and into the sea.

"Chief," I responded, like the goad that I was, "if that was a real threat, then I suggest you bring some big, strong guys, or you might find yourself trying to swim to shore."

He said nothing and walked away.

I immediately went to the bar and bought a bottle of Scotch—Dewar's if I recall—and grabbed two glasses. Then I went to the Captain's quarters and banged on the door. "Open up, Captain!" I shouted.

The Captain, Lars Engebretsen, answered the door and I walked into his living area. "We have to talk," I said, as I set the Scotch and two glasses in the middle of his coffee table.

"Okay," he said as I poured each of us a glass of straight whisky.

I proceeded to tell him of the Chief Engineer's comment and my reaction. Lars said not to worry about the chief; he was all talk and no action. Plus, if it came to that, he would put his money on me. "The Chief might find himself trying to swim to Miami."

Then we talked about the situation the company found itself in and possible ways to either increase revenue or reduce cost. We continued to talk, and drink, until three o'clock in the morning. We agreed later that, in our drunken states, we had both shared stories that could likely get each of us fired, and as such, that we had developed a bond of mutual trust.

Lars became a great friend and a great client. And he was instrumental in the success we had in implementing a variety of operating improvements across all the ships in their fleet.

In Chapter 2, the three case studies about leadership were titled: Gel the Team, Develop Allies, and Put Yourself Out There. Sometimes, as in the case of my evening with Lars, you can accomplish all three at once.

It is time to bring this book to a close. If you already are a card-carrying change agent, I hope that *Corporate Goad* has given you some new things to think about and some innovative ways to approach your work. If you are thinking about becoming an agent of change, whether as a management consultant or as part of an internal team or group that leads change initiatives, I hope that the book has been helpful in informing your decision.

This line of work is not for everyone. On one hand, it can be stimulating, engaging, and lucrative. But it can also be difficult, all-consuming, and very frustrating. It is perhaps best summed up by the words of Jerry Garcia of the Grateful Dead, "Somebody has to do something, and it's just incredibly pathetic that it has to be us."

ACKNOWLEDGMENTS

I owe my career to the many clients who gave me the opportunity to serve them. Their trust and confidence in me and my colleagues, and their willingness to tackle difficult and challenging problems, made them special people. I remember them all with respect and admiration.

In serving these clients, I was privileged to work with some of the smartest, most capable change agents in the business. On the dedication page, I named nineteen of my former partners who were the best of the best. But I was also blessed to have worked with and led at least two hundred outstanding staff members at Booz Allen. They produced some extraordinary work and, to a person, were true agents of change.

The life of a change agent is tough and demanding. There are many sacrifices that must be made. But the change agent's family is usually forced to make even more sacrifices: my wife, Bonita, and my three children, Katie, Anna, and Joseph, made major sacrifices to allow me to pursue my destiny. They took my long hours, missed dinners, and frequent absences from ball games and school plays in stride. That made the time I was able to be present all the more special. Bonita is a treasure and all three children are thriving and leading interesting lives, so I guess this didn't screw up the family too much.

Next, I need to acknowledge those people who were invaluable in helping me with the book. My editor, Matt Sharpe, is an amazing talent and a consummate professional. He shaped the manuscript into the book that it is today. Stewart Williams did an outstanding job on the cover and typography design. Rohit Bhargava, and his publishing company, IdeaPress, helped me get the book to market. Rohit has developed an interesting alternative to the traditional big house publishing model. I am lucky to be represented by him and IdeaPress Publishing.

Finally, I am very thankful to the twelve friends, former colleagues, and former clients who reviewed a draft of the book and provided constructive criticism and suggestions for improvement. They are: Ken Woodrow, the former President of Target Stores; Ed Mertz, the former General Manager of Buick Motor Division; Horst Metz, Frank Varasano, and Gary Shows, my partners at Booz Allen; Joe Fisher and Ferry de Bakker, my colleagues at Burson-Marsteller; Tony Castor, Managing Director and Senior Operating Partner at Kidd & Company; Dave Greene, former Young & Rubicam CFO and currently a Clinical Professor at the Kelley School of Business at Indiana University; my graduate school roommate and former VP of Finance at Rockwell, Jim Bachman; Dr. Jon Alspaugh, a recently reconnected friend from high school; and Katie Krauss, my daughter and a practicing change agent at Krayden, a global distribution company based in Denver.

BIBLIOGRAPHY

Carsalesbase.com. "Chrysler US Car Sales Figures." Accessed October 2017. www.carsalesbase.com/us-car-sales-data/chrysler/.

Collegeboard.org. "2014 College Board Results: SAT." Accessed May 2017. www.collegeboard.org/program-results/2014/sat.

Dictionary.com. "compartmentalization." 2017. Accessed June 2017. www.dictionary.com.

Dictionary.com. "process." 2017. Accessed June 2017. www.dictionary.com.

Dictionary.com. "protocol." 2017. Accessed April 2017. www.dictionary.com.

Dictionary.com. "unethical." 2017. Accessed May 2017. www.dictionary.com.

Dictionary.reverso.net. "specialization." 2017. Accessed June 2017. www.dictionary.reverso.net.

Kotter, John P. *Leading Change*. Boston: Harvard Business Review Press, 2012.

Krauss, Kurt and John Smith. "Rejecting Conventional Wisdom: How Academic Medical Centers Can Regain Their Leadership Positions." *Academic Medicine* 72, no. 7 (July 1997): 571-575.

Lathrop, J. Philip. *Restructuring Health Care: The Patient-Focused Paradigm*. San Francisco: Jossey-Bass, 1993.

Singer, Michael A. *The Untethered Soul*. Oakland, California: New Harbinger Publications, 2007.

Statista.com. "Luxury Car Market Share: United States 2016 Statistic." Accessed October 2017. www.statista.com/statistics/287620/luxury-vehicles-united-states-premium-vehicle-market-share/.

Stephens, Bret. "What Has Failed in France." *New York Times*, May 7, 2017.

Taylor, Larry. *Be An Orange*. Houston, Texas: Orange Press, 1992.

Tracy, Brian and Raul Villacis. *Change Agents*. Orlando, Florida: Celebrity Press, 2013.

White, Randy Wayne. *Bone Deep: A Doc Ford Novel*. New York: Putnam, 2014.

INDEX